WADSWORTH PHILOSOPHERS SERIES

ON

ADAM SMITH

Jack Russell Weinstein
California State University, Fresno

WADSWORTH
™
THOMSON LEARNING

Australia • Canada • Mexico • Singapore • Spain
United Kingdom • United States

For Gail: sixteen years and counting . . .

Printed in the United States of America
1 2 3 4 5 6 7 04 03 02 01 00

For permission to use material from this text, contact us:
Web: http://www.thomsonrights.com
Fax: 1-800-730-2215
Phone: 1-800-730-2214

For more information, contact:
Wadsworth/Thomson Learning, Inc.
10 Davis Drive
Belmont, CA 94002-3098
USA
http://www.wadsworth.com

ISBN: 0-534-58384-9

Table of Contents

Acknowledgements

Sections of this book have been published in modified forms as: "Guest Editor's Introduction: Critical Thinking and the Tradition of Political Philosophy — An Historical Overview." *Inquiry: Critical Thinking Across the Disciplines* vol. XVIII, no. 1 (Autumn, 1998): 4 – 21; "Critical Thinking and the Moral Sentiments: Adam Smith's Moral Psychology and Contemporary Debate in Critical Thinking and Informal Logic." *Inquiry: Critical Thinking Across the Disciplines* vol. XVI, no. 3 (Spring 1997): 78 – 91; the Boston University doctoral dissertation, *Adam Smith and the Problem of Neutrality in Contemporary Liberal Theory* (1997, UMI No. 9738666); and in the forthcoming, "Religion and Justice in the work of Adam Smith." *Kontroversen, Zeitschrift für Philosophie, Wissenschaft und Gesellschaft.* Heft 9, 2000.

I am also grateful to the members of the *New Jersey Regional Philosophy Association*, for their comments on my April, 1998 paper "Social Unity and the Moral Sentiments: Reclaiming Adam Smith", as well as to the invited members of the Liberty Fund Colloquium, "Adam Smith's System of Ordered Liberty" also held in April, 1998, in Chicago, Illinois.

Much of the section on Smith's life follows Ian Ross' *The Life of Adam Smith*. I am indebted to his excellent scholarship, particularly in matters pertaining to the scarce information on Smith's personality. I can only apologize if, after reading the first chapter, he is angered because I commandeered too many of the "good parts".

Charles L. Griswold Jr. has been a wonderful guide through the world of Adam Smith, both as my professor at Boston University, and as a mentor. I thank him for all his lessons and for his permission to use the term "protreptic" as prominently as I have. I am also grateful to Daniel Kolak, General Editor of *The Wadsworth Philosophers Series*, for giving me the opportunity to be a part of his project.

The core of this book was presented under the title "The Road Not Taken: Rediscovering Adam Smith" as part of the Spring, 2000 Colloquium of the Department of Philosophy at California State University, Fresno. The questions asked of me by the attendees have played an important role in my presentation of the arguments. I appreciate the interest and attention of the colloquium audience, all of whom had the kindness to sit through a discussion that extended well beyond acceptable time limits.

Drafts of chapters or of the entire manuscript have been commented on by my colleagues at CSU Fresno: Karen Bell, Otávio Bueno, Warren Kessler, and Terry Winant. I am grateful for their efforts. Two undergraduates were kind enough to act as guinea pigs; I thank Jon Petty and Joy Plummer for their assistance. My father, Mark Weinstein, was invaluable in his reading of my work, as always. His ability to spot my weakest and most polemic statements continues to be both impressive and relieving. I remain appreciative as always. Kim Donehower was the first to read the manuscript and was also my most immediate supplier of intellectual energy and emotional support. I thank her for her help.

Finally, with her reading of the manuscript, Gail Sherman Reilly acted as the representative for the world outside *academe*. I thank her for her efforts and for all her faith in me throughout the years. I could not have asked for a more supportive, caring, and perceptive friend. Her advice and encouragement have been a major inspiration for sixteen years. Dedicating this book to her cannot adequately express my love and admiration for her, but at least it's a start.

Key to Abbreviations

Astronomy   *The Principles Which Lead and Direct Philosophical Enquires Illustrated by the History of Astronomy*, from *EPS*.

Corr.   *Correspondence of Adam Smith*. Ed. E.C. Mossner and I.S. Ross. Indianapolis: Liberty Press, 1987.

EPS   *Essays on Philosophical Subjects*. Ed. W.P.D. Wightman and J.C. Bryce. Indianapolis: Liberty Press, 1982.

LJ   *Lectures on Jurisprudence*. Ed. R.L. Meek and D.D. Raphael. Indianapolis: Liberty Press, 1982.

LJ(A)   *Lecture on Jurisprudence*, dated 1762 - 3, from *LJ*

LJ(B)   *Lecture on Jurisprudence,* dated 1766, from *LJ*.

LRBL   *The Lectures on Rhetoric and Belles Lettres*. Ed. J.C. Bryce. Indianapolis: Liberty Press, 1985.

TMS   *Theory of Moral Sentiments*. Ed. A.L. Macfie and D.D. Raphael. Indianapolis: Liberty Press, 1982

WN   *An Inquiry into the Nature and Causes of the Wealth of Nations*. 2 vols. Ed. R.H. Campbell and A.S. Skinner. Indianapolis: Liberty Press, 1976.

Whenever possible, Smith's works are referred to via parenthetical citations. Unless otherwise noted, the citation refers to the text that is the main subject of the discussion the citation is located in. When citations refer to other texts, abbreviations will be provided.

1
Introduction

Why read Adam Smith? For most of today's readers, the answer is historical. Smith is an important figure in the history of economics, and although many of his theories have been modified or rejected, reading Smith adds insight into the evolution of economics. In this regard, students and scholars read Smith in order to learn more about his influence. Others read Smith because they are devout capitalists. Smith has become an icon for greed and self-interest, and many look to him for justification of such practices. In this regard, many read Smith for legitimation. Still others read Smith because they are anti-capitalists. Smith has become an icon for greed and self-interest, and many look to him as a symbol to condemn. In this regard, Smith serves as a convenient enemy. Finally, many read Smith simply because he is important. They might not understand why, but they seek to fill gaps in their knowledge. In this regard, Smith fulfills one's intellectual curiosity. This is not a complete list of reasons, but I suspect it covers the most common motivations.

These reasons all have two things in common. First, they treat Smith as an economist, and second, they value Smith for that which he has already accomplished. This book challenges both those assumptions. This book treats Smith not as an economist who happened to write philosophy, but, rather, as a philosopher who wrote some

1

economics. Before he wrote *An Inquiry into the Nature and Causes of the Wealth of Nations*, Smith examined moral theory, rhetoric, and philosophy of science. His first book, *The Theory of Moral Sentiments*, made him famous, and Smith's ethical theory is currently experiencing a revival owing to a group of committed scholars who seek to renew interest in many different aspects of his work.

This book does not treat Smith as an historical curiosity who has accomplished all that he was capable of. It treats Smith as someone with a contemporary message. That capitalism is the dominant political system in the contemporary world is almost without doubt. That capitalism is *succeeding*, however, is much more contentious. I will argue that Smith would challenge such claims of success. As the standard of living rises in most of the world, few could challenge the notion that vast numbers of people are being left behind. While some countries gorge themselves into obesity, others starve. Furthermore, while the information revolution has made access to recorded knowledge easier than ever, global cultural experience is becoming whitewashed in a money- and media-driven frenzy of homogeneity. Every generation has complained that their successors are intellectually inferior and poorly educated. Sometimes the weaker of us are forced to wonder whether *this time* it might be true.

Smith's work addresses all of these issues. His free-market structure – Smith never uses the term *capitalism* – is designed to supply all members of the community with all appropriate resources and education. Smith suggests that difficulties in providing necessities are indicative of moral choices made by the community. He argues that injustices are always ethical problems before they are economic. Smith spent his life endeavoring to show that economics must be presented alongside ethics, and that the two cannot ignore each other. He believed that there must be governmental mechanisms to support those who need them. For Smith, equality of opportunity is not merely a lack of barriers towards resources, but also active participation in providing assistance to those who are denied those resources. Smith is neither libertarian nor radically *laissez faire*. While his critics offer important challenges, they are nevertheless rarely correct in attributing that which they challenge to Smith. In this book, I will explain the connections Smith found between economics and ethics, and I will outline Smith's argument showing how each supports the other.

This book is introductory. It assumes no prior knowledge of Smith. However, the reader should not be tempted into thinking that it is uncontroversial. Introductory books are inevitably laden with biased agendas. In such books, there is rarely enough space or detail in which to enumerate competing interpretations or their respective merits. The beginning reader is generally excluded from controversy. In many ways, this book is no exception. It assumes that which is the most hotly debated topic in Smith scholarship: that Smith's work is systematic. The presentation is designed to show the reader not only how Smith's writings are connected, but how they complement each other.

Traditionally, Smith studies have been plagued by an interpretive difficulty commonly referred to as *The Adam Smith Problem,* the essence of which is the assertion that *TMS* and *WN* are incompatible. The argument contends that *TMS*, Smith's first book, is founded on the claim that humans are motivated by altruism, and that *WN*, Smith's second book, is founded on the claim that humans are motivated by self-interest. Naturally, two such theories would be mutually exclusive, and therein lies the problem. Were this the case, Smith's work could never be systematic; it would be inconsistent. The consequence of the Adam Smith Problem is that one is forced to choose one work over the other – one could not accept both – and this, in turn, leaves the other behind. Traditionally, *WN* has been chosen over *TMS*.

For the most part, the Adam Smith Problem has been rejected in most contemporary Smith scholarship. It is too simplistic and it is based on a misreading of Smith's work. Neither book claims that *all* human actions share the same motivation, only that *some* actions are motivated by self-interest while *others* are motivated by altruism. As Smith rightly understood, moral psychology is too complex to be reduced to one universal cause. The Adam Smith Problem also misunderstands Smith's most central term 'sympathy', a term that is mistakenly identified as a synonym for beneficence. Sympathy is not to be equated with altruism. It is to be understood as a method of understanding and communicating any emotion. The mechanics of sympathy will be discussed in detail.

Nevertheless, suspicions regarding a systematic reading of Smith remain, and in this book, I challenge those suspicions. In this book Smith's works are presented in their relationship to each other, and I offer explicit discussions regarding where connections are found. I am also generous with my textual citations so that Smith's own voice is always present, and so that skeptical readers can challenge the reliability of my claims by examining the relevant passages themselves.

Rather than divide Smith's system by theme, with one notable exception, I have chosen to highlight each work separately in order to retain the integrity of each text, and to help remind readers of the role of interpretation. *Adam Smith,* D.D. Raphael's important introductory text, is divided into chapters titled "Ethics", "Economics", and others of similar name.[1] For the most part, I choose not to do that. Dividing Smith's work by topic may connote the separateness of those fields. I wish to advance a more systematic understanding of Smith's writing. In dividing the chapters by text, I wish to challenge the notion that each work discusses only one topic, and I also hope to ensure that readers remain oriented to whatever work is being emphasized at the time. Only in the last chapter do I focus explicitly on one topic. By that time, the reader should be familiar enough with the exchange between texts, that a more topical approach is appropriate. However, even in that last chapter, one text remains the primary focus.

The first chapter discusses Smith's life and his philosophical influences. Most of his biographical information comes from accounts others have given, and little is known regarding Smith's innermost thoughts. Therefore, this first chapter must rely primarily on anecdotes and observations. This introduces an important theme: readers are forced to understand someone in terms of how *others* see that person. This is essential for Smith's system. For Smith, self-identity is at least partially constructed by how one is viewed by others. One must therefore learn how to interpret the account of the witness. In this first chapter, I also introduce the relationship between Smith and his dear friend David Hume. This highlights a second theme, that of relationships. I suggest that Smith's philosophy is that which it is because of Smith's deep regard for his friendships. He has great faith in the affection of others and the way in which one's community cultivates morality and personal commitment through care. I illustrate this care with accounts of Smith and Hume's interaction.

The second chapter discusses Smith's earliest known work, *The Principles Which Lead and Direct Philosophical Enquires Illustrated by the History of Astronomy*. In this part of the book, I explicitly enumerate difficulties in interpreting Smith. Here, the reader is introduced to a central problem in Smith scholarship: much of what readers rely on for understanding Smith was not authored by him. Sets of student notes are used to elaborate on ambiguities left in Smith's work because Smith died before he could complete his planned system. Student notes are emphasized a second time in chapter five, a much shorter chapter in which I focus on Smith's conception of justice. Again, at that point, the reader should be familiar enough with Smith's work to see the process of interpretation more explicitly. The two middle chapters focus on Smith's published works and the connections between the two. Although *The Theory of Moral Sentiments* and *Inquiry into the Nature and Causes of the Wealth of Nations* are each treated in their own chapter, emphasis is placed upon their unity, especially in chapter four. Also, in the two middle chapters, I refer to the recent work of John Rawls. Because I wish to argue that Smith has contemporary relevance, Smith's work must be compared to Rawls'. Rawls' 1971 book *A Theory of Justice* has been so influential that no political theory can be evaluated without taking it into consideration. However, no prior knowledge of Rawls is necessary for that discussion. Finally, I conclude the book with some suggestions as to what today's readers might learn from reconsidering Smith in light of a systematic reading or his work.

A preparatory note on the use of language throughout this book: although I retain the original spelling and grammar in all of Smith's quotes, where I do not quote him directly, I modernize his language. The most obvious example of this is the removal of gender-bias. Although Smith uses the masculine pronoun to represent all people, I have opted for the more inclusive practice of using the masculine and feminine pronouns. My doing so sidesteps a conversation regarding the propriety of taking an Enlightenment text and disregarding whatever biases are inherent in the eighteenth century worldview. It might be suggested that my removal of the gender-bias is a misrepresentation of Smith's shortcomings. This objection deserves to be addressed. Unfortunately, space considerations do not allow such a discussion here. I ask that the reader be aware of the consciousness of my rhetorical decision, and to give Smith's theory the benefit of the doubt, if only for the time being.[2] In many different respects, Smith is most often categorized in terms of being *one of us*, or *one of them*. I therefore ask my audience to put these prejudices aside as much as possible. He has much to offer, and it is rarely what one expects.

2

Life and Influences

Descriptions of Adam Smith are mostly unflattering but rarely offered without affection. His friends, peers and acquaintances provide accounts of him that are mixtures of deprecating humor, respect, and care. Like Smith's own philosophy, the anecdotes that inform us about him contain a complex mixture of self-interestedness on the part of the story teller – the stories almost always portray Smith in a less than ideal light, primarily for the sake of the entertainment of the story tellers and their audiences – and a hefty but subtle dose of sympathy. Despite the often caricature-like nature of these stories, it is hard to doubt that Smith was likeable and worthy of intellectual admiration. Clearly, he was a good and compassionate man who loved both the social and the intellectual pleasures.

Not much is known of Smith's most personal thoughts. Although he corresponded with friends throughout his life, his letters betray few intimate feelings. We must therefore be satisfied with descriptions and not admissions. Adam Smith was said to have a large nose and big teeth. He spoke with a harsh voice and sometimes stammered. At social gatherings, he was more disposed to lecture than engage in conversation, but sought out the company of others and belonged to many social clubs. Smith was reported to walk "with a strange gait, his head moving in a gentle manner from side to side, and his body swaying 'vermicularly'... as if with each step he meant to alter his direction, or even turn back'". He was known to walk carrying his cane over his shoulder, "as a soldier carries his musket".[3]

Smith, although reserved, was not without opinion. One commentator described him as "extremely communicative...[he] delivered himself, on every subject with a freedom, and even boldness, quite opposite to the apparent reserve of his appearance."[4] According to Alexander Carlyle, who shared membership with Smith at the Poker Club:

> He was the most absent man in Company that I ever saw, Moving his Lips and talking to himself and Smiling, in the midst of large Company's. If you awak'd him from his Reverie, and made him attend to the subject of conversation, he immediately began a Harangue and never stop'd till he told you all he knew about it, with the utmost Philosophical Ingenuity.[5]

Smith's absent mindedness is legendary. He once fell into a tannery vat full of fat while he was preoccupied with an impromptu lecture on the division of labor. He walked 15 miles in his dressing gown in "a fit of abstraction".[6] There is an account of him, while working at the Customs House, unknowingly but scrupulously imitating someone else's signature on a government document, simply because that person had signed on the sheet immediately before Smith began to sign his own name. Lady George Lennox, who described Smith as "the most Absent Man who ever lived", described a morning visit in which,

> falling into discourse, Mr. Smith took a piece of bread and butter, which, after he had rolled round and round, he put into the teapot and pour'd water upon it; some time after he poured it into a cup, and when he had tasted it, he said it was the worst tea he had ever met with.[7]

The picture we have of Smith, then, is of a physically unattractive, absent-minded, shy man with a funny walk, but such a portrait does not do credit to the affection others felt for him. Biographer Ian Ross, tells of the paradigmatic evolution of Mme Riccoboni's affection for the philosopher. Although she found him "ugly as the devil" at first, "the goodness of his heart won her over", and eventually, she wished "the devil would carry off all the *gens de lettres*" and bring Smith back to her.[8] There is another report of Smith

7

being embarrassed by an English woman's direct and persistent unwelcome amorous advances; he was not without admirers.

Smith was beloved by many companions, and by his students. He had numerous life-long friendships and traveled among some of the most famous minds of his time, including, but not limited to Edmund Burke, Benjamin Franklin, Adam Ferguson, Turgot, and Voltaire. His closest friend, and perhaps his greatest influence, was David Hume, whose last writing was a letter to Smith.

Smith was a student of Francis Hutcheson at the University of Glasgow. He corresponded with Immanuel Kant, and had a tumultuous interaction with Samuel Johnson. Smith's loyalty to Hume is shown in the report that Smith once called Dr. Johnson a "son of a bitch" – a very bold statement for the time – after Johnson had publicly insulted Hume.[9] From a certain perspective, one might claim that Smith had the last word in that argument, since Johnson was later quoted as saying, "Sir, I was once in company with Smith, and we did not take to each other, but had I known that he loved rhyme [poetry] as much as you tell me he does, I should have hugged him."[10]

Smith's last words were addressed to his friends. Henry MacKenzie reports him, on his death bed, as saying, "I love your company, gentlemen, but I must leave you to go to another world." James Hutton, Smith's literary executor, records Smith's words differently. According to Hutton, Smith expired after uttering, "I believe we must adjourn this meeting to some other place."[11] In either case, it is clear that Smith had great esteem for personal relationships, a fact that makes its way into the very core of Smith's moral philosophy.

Smith never married. He is rumored to have had one, maybe two loves in his life, but nothing came of them. Ross argues that Smith was comfortable with being a bachelor, but there is enough evidence to suggest that Smith missed having a family of his own. He went out of his way to initiate relationships with younger people, acted as advisor to students, and was extremely charitable to the distant youth in his family; Smith was an only child. He accepted the position of traveling tutor, taking responsibility for bringing the Duke of Baccleugh into manhood, and, eventually, advising the young man through the earliest periods of his marriage. Smith was often seen walking in the company of a young blind boy – Smith took responsibility for the child's education, and helped him enter the University of Glasgow. As Ross himself points out, Smith, in a letter written at the age of 54, seemed to retain the hope of one day having children himself.[12] It is possible that Smith was not that comfortable in his bachelorhood, after all. In Smith's writing, especially in his comments on education, we see a paternal tendency and a deep care for the younger generation that may have been the closest to a child-rearing experience that Smith could come.

Of course, Smith is known for his ideas, not his personality. He was a diligent and conscientious worker, and was well rewarded for his efforts. As a student, he was the recipient of many awards that would assist him though his schooling. As he grew older, Smith's writing and teaching met with great praise. He was a university professor, a professional private tutor, and was eventually appointed Lord Rector of the University of Glasgow. *TMS* went though six editions during his lifetime, and *WN* went through four. Each was extremely well received, and each was translated into numerous languages almost immediately upon publication.

Smith's rewards were social as well as professional. His fame preceded him in his European travels, and his reputation allowed him access to the most active minds of his time. Smith even found his way, as a character, into two dialogues written by Adam Ferguson, a contemporary with whom Smith had a difficult, but ultimately very caring relationship. One anecdote illustrates the respect that the intellectual community had for Smith:

> There was an Edinburgh tradition that on one occasion during [a] London visit Smith was one of the last gentlemen to come into the room in Dundas's Wimbleton villa, when [William] Pitt [MP], [William] Grenville [MP, later the first Baron of Grenville], Henry Addington [MP, later a Prime Minister], and William Wilberforce [MP] were other guests, The company rose to receive Smith, and he asked them to be seated. Pitt is represented as saying: 'No, we will stand till you are first seated, for we are all your scholars'.[13]

Despite his success, Smith's work came at a great price. He was a sickly child, who suffered from a lifetime of psychosomatic illnesses triggered by the stress of composition. He would often be forced to stop writing because of sudden bouts of an illnesses diagnosed simply as "hypochondriasis". By all accounts, including his own, his poor-health impinged on his work time, delaying completion of his projects for much longer than he would have hoped.

Writing was not easy for Smith. He wrote of himself, "I am a slow a very slow workman, who do and undo everything I write at least a half dozen times before I can be tolerably pleasd with it." (*Corr.* 276) Much of this delay was due to physical difficulties and Smith often found it necessary to hire an amanuesis to whom he would dictate. Apparently, while dictating *WN*, Smith was in the habit of "rubbing his head against the wall above the chimney piece."[14] Supposedly, marks from his wig remained until the wall was repainted.

Smith also paid a social price for his work. He spent much of his life moving away from and then returning to his mother, the most lengthy and influential relationship in Smith's life. Margaret Douglas, Smith's mother, died at the remarkable age of ninety, only a few years before Smith himself passed away. It is both impossible and undesirable to deconstruct what effect his relationship with his mother had on his romantic life. Preemptively, we can observe, that Smith seemed to have as good relationships with women as his time and stature would have allowed. He was, for example, a welcome visitor among the "great ladies" of Paris. He was also quite close to his cousin, Janet Douglas, who lived with Smith and his mother for a very long time. It is through his cousin that we see Smith confront most explicitly his virtually non-existent romantic life. Upon being reunited with his one old love, Janet is said to have asked a "beaming" but silent Smith, "Do you not know, Adam, this is your ain Jeannie?" but Smith did nothing more than remained smiling "gently", and nothing further is reported of the incident.[15] Smith remained a bachelor his entire life, and placed whatever creative desire he had for progeny into a legacy of written works that has been influential far beyond what he could have estimated. It is this fact that leads Ross to quip, "It is feared that the biographer can do little more with the topic of Smith's sex life than contribute a footnote to the history of sublimation."[16]

Margaret Douglas Smith was already a widow when Adam Smith was born in Kirkaldy, Scotland in 1723. Her husband had died shortly after Adam was conceived. At the time, Scotland was under an ambiguous political transition. Sixteen years earlier, the small country had finally lost its independence. This culminated four hundred years of periodic and brutal war against the British, and one hundred years of resisting the political ramifications of the unification of the British and Scottish royal families. Acceptance of the final treaty hinged in no small part on the threat of trade sanctions against the nobility who had themselves lost large sums of money in an attempt to colonize Central America.

Scotland was a mixture of intellectual and aristocratic privilege, and poor laboring classes. It was mostly rural, and the main industries of Kirkaldy were coal mining and salt panning, but an incredibly influential industry, the manufacture of nails, held a vital place in the economy since many workers were given nails as wages and would exchange them for goods in lieu of money. This phenomenon of exchanging surplus goods in lieu of money would figure prominently in *WN*.

Smith came from a landowning family, but they were not wealthy. It is reasonable to assume that he himself must have struggled with identity issues. In addition to whatever stigma he felt from his appearance, his stammering and his odd tendencies to withdraw in social situations, Smith was still Glasgow and Oxford educated. While no doubt feeling some sense of superiority over the working classes, he too faced the difficulties of class difference and of being some form of an outcast. The Scottish intellectual elite, while being among the most active in the world, felt inferior to the intelligentsia in England. In order to minimize their Scottish identity, they often referred to themselves as "North Britons" and not as Scots.[17] Those who were able, struggled to imitate British accents in order to appear more sophisticated. After returning from his studies in Oxford, Smith was complemented for "his pronunciation and his style [which] were much superior to what could...be acquired in Scotland only."[18] Ironically, Smith was not very pleased with his experiences in England. His personal correspondences, and remarks about the institutions of education in his published work, show explicitly that he was unsatisfied, if not bitter, regarding the quality of instruction at Oxford.

Many of these themes figure prominently in Smith's work: the ability to synthesize manners, the economic value of goods, the vast difference in educational opportunities in the classes, and the role and influence of trade in governance. Jerry Muller argues that being Scottish was very much an advantage to Smith since he was able to have the benefit of British education while not being blinded by the "English intellectual provincialism" that viewed "British liberty as ...[a]... unique historical legacy".[19] Walter Bagehot, one hundred years after *WN*'s publication, wrote that Smith's project showed "how, from being a savage, man rose to become a Scotchman".[20]

Not much is known of Smith's childhood. Most famously, the three-year-old Smith is said to have been kidnapped by gypsies. He was found a few miles down the road, according to one version of the story, and was returned to his mother unharmed. We also know that Smith excelled at school in even his earliest of years. Dugald Stewart, Smith's student and biographer, wrote:

> Among those companions of his earliest years, Mr. Smith soon attracted notice by his passion for books, and by the extraordinary powers of his memory. The weakness of his bodily constitutions

prevented him from partaking in their more active amusements, but he was much beloved by them on account of his temper, which, though warm, was to an uncommon degree friendly and generous. Even then he was remarkable for those habits which remained with him through his life, of speaking to himself when alone, and of *absence* in company.[21]

Smith's intellectual talents were evident at an early age, as was his ability to use his sentiments – his friendliness and his warmth – to bond with others. After the small burgh school of Kirkaldy, Smith continued his studies at the University of Glasgow and then, eventually at Oxford University. In 1746, Smith left Oxford, returned to Kirkaldy, then two years later, was asked to give a series of public lectures in Edinburgh. Manuscripts of later versions of these lectures were found in 1930, and their content will be discussed in the next chapter. For the moment, it is sufficient to indicate that their topic was literary style and methods of communication. This too will be an important theme in Smith's work.

The success of Smith's Edinburgh Lectures – E.G. West suggests that each lecture had about 100 persons in attendance – was essential both for Smith's financial security since he was paid per student, and for his professional success.[22] Perhaps as a direct result of his new reputation, Smith was asked to accept the chair of Logic at Glasgow University. It was through the Edinburgh lectures and his tenure at Glasgow that Smith became acquainted with the intelligentsia of the day, and it was during this time that Smith's thought matured enough to form the basis of what would become his first book.

Smith wrote two published books in his lifetime, the first, *TMS*, during his tenure at Glasgow, the second, *WN*, quite some time after he left. Smith resigned from the university and was hired as a traveling tutor for the Duke of Baccleugh, and prepared his economic treatise while he traveled. After retuning from Paris and then London, Smith lived with his mother in Kirkaldy and then again in London. In 1778, Smith accept an appointment as Commissioner of Customs for Scotland, and moved to Canongate, with his mother and Janet Douglas. During that time, and after their deaths, Smith continued to revise his works. He lived to see the publication of the sixth edition of *TMS* and the fourth edition of *WN*. His mother died in 1784, Janet Douglas died in 1788, and Smith himself passed away in 1790.

Intellectually, Smith was an important figure in the Scottish Enlightenment, an intellectual movement of the eighteenth century that, among its characteristics, seemed, at least according to Alasdair

MacIntyre, to unify popular governance and intellectual activity. MacIntyre writes:

> The effect was to create that very rare phenomenon, an educated public, in this case a philosophically educated public, which shared standards of rational justification and a shared deference to a teaching authority, that of the professors of philosophy and especially of moral philosophy. To be called to account for one's beliefs and judgments, in respect either of their justification by deduction from first principles or of the evidentness of those first principles themselves, was a matter from about 1730 onward of being called upon to defend oneself in the forums of philosophically educated option, rather than in the courts of the church.[23]

The size of the educated 'public' MacIntyre alludes to is questionable since clearly, the laboring classes did not have the same opportunities as the landowners. The two classes were not educated in the same manner and most people were on the very edges of illiteracy.[24] MacIntyre makes more of this than he should. However, Smith clearly had great faith in everyone's capacity for, and the restorative powers of, education, as well as the ability of all individuals to participate unashamedly in the decisions that contributed both to personal and common good.

MacIntyre is correct in pointing out that the role of the public in legislation and moral adjudication were central concerns of the Scottish enlightenment, as was the relationship of all of these to science. Two central debates raged among the Scottish thinkers. First, the Scots investigated the connection between science and human activity. Like other Enlightenment thinkers, they were deeply affected by Newton's discoveries that the laws of the heavens are the same as the laws of earth. They sought the most scientific explanations in which to describe and prescribe human interaction and moral adjudication. Yet, at the same time, they struggled with a second debate, the relationship between history and philosophical thought: is history prescriptive or simply informative? As Knud Haakonssen writes:

> The new social and contextual history saw the explanation of nature as an integral part of polite culture and of the culture of the mind. This work made clear the full extent of the teleological and providentialist twist put on Newtonianism, and this again made better appreciation of how Newton was extended to the moral

sphere. Science served better than anything to show humanity its place and its function in the general order instituted by the Divinity and science was therefore itself part of the practical moralizing. At the same time, the 'mental sciences' could work out the details of the moral psychology that made moralizing possible.[25]

History was, for Smith, a central component of moral theory "because moral consciousness, moral judgment, and moral institutions were formed by the accommodations reached at a given stage of society and in a given type of government."[26] History is essential, both in political and personal development. Knowledge of self and others, or, in other words, personal history and the awareness of the personal history of others, becomes that which enables moral adjudication. *The Theory of Moral Sentiments* is founded on an awareness of the need to know one's own, and other people's stories. In *WN,* Smith argues that economic systems are based upon a four-stage theory of history. For Smith, political structure, economic theory, and history are intertwined.

The Scottish Enlightenment is the umbrella that unifies Smith's greatest influences. First, his teacher, Francis Hutcheson and Hutcheson's own great influence Lord Shaftesbury, then Smith's best friend and philosophical advisor, David Hume. A complete account of Smith's influences would require a discussion of Mandeville and Hobbes whom he wrote against, as well as the Stoics. The former two will be discussed in the third chapter of this book. Stoicism will be touched upon shortly and then revisited throughout the third chapter as well. The remainder of this chapter will focus on the work of Shaftesbury, Hutcheson, and Hume.

The first philosopher of concern is Anthony Ashley Cooper, third Earl of Shaftesbury (1671 – 1713). Shaftesbury, as he is referred to, is a typical Scottish Enlightenment figure, although he was British. He relies on reason, and aims to divorce moral philosophy from religion. Morality is a 'natural' project and is to be understood as using scientific principles and methodologies. It is best developed within a community and independent of dogma. This is not to suggest that God plays no role for either Shaftesbury or for the other thinkers of the time. The role of God is complex in Shaftesbury, as it is for Smith, and Smith takes great pains to distinguish between human psychological phenomena and "the Author of Nature".

Shaftesbury was the first philosopher to use the term 'moral sense'. This phrase, which would be all-important to Smith's development, refers to an internal awareness of virtue, and of right and wrong. Shaftesbury was an important influence on Smith, although Smith would challenge the existence of the moral sense. It is worth remarking that influence is not a synonym for agreement. Those who oppose philosophers are often noticeably influenced by the disagreements between them.

The term moral sense is most easily thought of in terms of an internal sense. It may *prima facie* be understood as a complement to the five vehicles of empirical knowledge, and may also, *prima facie,* be related to Locke's 'reflection', that which allows a person to combine the simple ideas of sense data into complex ideas. However, moral sense is more than this, and should not be seen as simply a substitute for a Lockean epistemological tool. For Shaftesbury, although the capacity for moral judgment is hard-wired into all humans, the moral sense needs to be cultivated; it is not strictly intuition. The reader of the moral sense theorists would be well-served to remember that although most people are born with the capacity to see, the ability to appreciate beauty, art, and visual sophistication is the product of discipline, attention, and education. It is useful to think of morality in aesthetic terms. For Shaftesbury, as well as for Hutcheson and Smith, morality operates in similar ways to our experience of beauty, harmony, and proportion.

The moral sense is said to be cultivated through reason and through sociality. For Shaftesbury, use of the moral sense is learned, to some degree from others, and it is only truly realized when one come to an accurate understanding of him- or herself. Free inquiry is the key to self-awareness, even if such inquiry is to examine forbidden topics such as atheism. Shaftesbury argued that human nature was ultimately benevolent, and that such motives could guide one's intellectual endeavors. In *Advice to an Author*, Shaftesbury writes:

> And thus at least we are returned to our old article of advice: that main preliminary of self-study and inward converse which we have found so much wanting in the authors of our time. They should add the wisdom of the heart to the task and exercise the brain, in order to bring proportion and beauty into their works. That their composition and vein of writing may be natural and free, they should settle matters in the first place with themselves.[27]

It is through Hutcheson, the immediate intellectual heir to Shaftesbury, that the notion of moral sense was transmitted to Smith. Hutcheson (1694 – 1746), who was Irish, not Scottish, taught at the

University of Glasgow and was a follower Shaftesbury. While a student at Glasgow, Smith probably heard Hutcheson lecture on ethics three days per week, and then was probably tested twice more per week, in Latin, on the subjects of Hutcheson's morning course. Smith might also have joined Hutcheson's 'private' course twice a week, and also joined the prelection for Hutcheson's main course on jurisprudence and politics five days per week.[28] Hutcheson lectured in English and had a lively style. He walked away from the podium and moved throughout the classroom while he spoke. Smith is said to have tried to imitate Hutcheson's style during his earliest forays into lecturing, but abandoned it and found his own.

Hutcheson, a former Presbyterian minister in Ulster, followed Shaftesbury's philosophy in several ways. First, he argued for knowledge of Good and Evil as independent of knowledge of God. Second, he argued that the happiness of others is important to morality. Hutcheson is ultimately utilitarian in many regards, arguing that the best happiness is that which results in the greatest good for the greatest numbers. Third, and most important, for Smith, Hutcheson sought to take Shaftesbury's rather vague notion of the moral sense and develop it into a coherent and defensible philosophical system.

For Hutcheson, reason cannot dictate whether an action is virtuous. We may suggest that an action is virtuous because it is beneficent, but why is beneficence moral? Ultimately, for Hutcheson, actions are virtuous because they please, although they need not please the actor. They may please an altogether different person. Furthermore, although the moral sense may be cultivated by education and reason, it cannot be created. Education and reason can only improve that which already exists. Hutcheson believed that he had supplied a definition of virtue as well as a motivation for acting virtuously. A person is acting virtuously when their actions please someone, and they chose to act virtuously because it pleases them to please others.[29]

These arguments lead directly into Smith's theorizing about the moral sentiments, and set the foundation for his theory of sympathy and the impartial spectator. They also define a great deal of Smith's problematic. Critics of Hutcheson might argue that his moral sense contains too much ambiguity. Suppose, for example, hurting others is pleasing to someone. Would this count as a virtuous act? Suppose also that a moral actor is mistaken in what he or she regards as virtuous. Is this a blameworthy act or a praiseworthy one? These are difficulties that Smith himself struggled with throughout his life.

The beginning of the answer to both of these questions rests in the Stoic doctrine of self-command, the belief that it is virtuous to keep one's emotions regulated. This notion is a descendant of the classical Greek virtue *sophrosune,* which is often translated as either temperance or moderation, and which implies a strong foundation of accurate self-knowledge. Its systematic origins are found in Plato and Aristotle and extended discussions can be found in Plato's dialogues *Charmides* and *Phaedrus,* as well as in Aristotle's *Nicomachean Ethics.* However, for the Scottish Enlightenment thinkers, self-command emphasizes control of one's emotions, and in that regard, self-command is a Stoic conception.

The Stoics sought to enumerate the law of nature and to use it as a standard for human political and moral activities. In this regard alone, there is a direct link from the Stoics to the Scottish Enlightenment. Stoicism can be traced back as early as Heraclitus (c540 B.C.E. to c480 B.C.E.) but is most widely understood as a later Hellenistic and Roman philosophy whose most famous adherents are Digoenes of Seleucia (c 320), Panaetius of Rhodes (c185 B.C.E – 110 B.C.E.), Posidonius of Apamea (c135 – c51), Seneca (4 B.C.E – 65), Epictetus (c50-c138), and the emperor Marcus Aurelius (121-180). Smith illustrates Stoic principles using Epictetus and Aurelius.

The Stoics believed that the universe was synonymous with God and had order. Change followed natural laws and, in that regard, since the natural law was constant, there was, in some sense, both change and continuity. Humans held a particular place in the system since, as rational beings, they most resembled the universe in its totality, but each creature, including humans, had responsibilities towards one another. Four cardinal virtues governed Stoic ethics: intelligence, bravery, justice and self-control. Each virtue contains an element of intelligence – for example, bravery involves knowing that which one should fear, and justice requires knowing that which rightfully belongs to others – and each has a strong element of control. After knowledge of that which is right is attained, one must have enough control to act appropriately based upon that knowledge. For Smith, the two cardinal virtues are also self-knowledge and self-command. Smith's economic system, in particular his discussion of the informative aspect of natural price, is, in some way, an attempt to add the Stoic notion of intelligence to a market system based upon desire.

A central tension in Stoic thought is the relationship between independence and dependence. Nature has its rules that all creatures and all of their acts follow. However, rational creatures can reflect on their action and choose those actions that are moral, rejecting those that are not. There is great difficulty then, in discovering that which is truly in one's own power, and that which is only inadvertent adherence to the *logos*, a term that is most often translated as word, order, or, in some loose sense, logic. The stoics argued that self-knowledge and self-command would, in combination with the study of physics and metaphysics, lead to an awareness of *logos* that would then guide each person's actions, and that acting in accordance with the natural law was acting in harmony with nature. For the Stoics, to act following nature is to act ethically. The Stoics also had great faith that since the universe was governed by natural law, good was always possible, even out of evil, and that seemingly bad acts lead to good results. Here, in the claim that the order of nature can guide even vicious actions towards virtue, we see an anticipation of Smith's most famous metaphor, the invisible hand.

This notion of harmony through order is, in some important sense, a rejection of the validity of emotions since, for many, emotions are regarded as irrational. The Stoics argued that one should control his or her emotions, and that one should reject vanity and pride; anger is self-destructive. Temperance of anger, disappointment, grief, or other similar emotions is a recognition that actions turn out for the best. It is faith in the ultimate order of nature. These themes are all found in Smith. Yet, for Smith, emotions continue to play an important part in his moral system. After all, Smith does offer a theory of moral *sentiments* and not a theory of the moral *sense*. For Smith, the Stoic doctrine of harmony of nature and reason evolves into a harmony between emotions and people, and the Stoic doctrine of self-command is that which Smith develops into an emotional self-control that is necessary for any praiseworthy action. Furthermore, the harmony of self-interest leads to the benefit of others. Without such harmony, the self-interest of the butcher, the brewer, and the baker would do little for anyone other than the butcher, the brewer and the baker.

As an enumeration of Smith's influences, the above might present a conflict. On the one hand, Smith was influenced by the moral sense theorists, yet he himself puts forth a theory of moral sentiment. On the other hand, he builds on Shatftesbury and Hutcheson's account of the role of emotion in moral theory, yet he is influenced by the Stoic doctrine that rejects emotions in moral adjudication. These tensions can be resolved only by discussing Smith's work in detail, and not in a preparatory first chapter such as this one. I will provide such a discussion in the following chapters. However, one last piece of the puzzle must be introduced before we advance to a more detailed discussion, and that is the influence of David Hume.

Smith met Hume while he was in Edinburgh lecturing on rhetoric. They became life-long friends. Hume died on August 25, 1776, and of the 168 Smith letters catalogued through the day Hume died, 54 are either to or from Hume. This make letters to and from Hume constitute almost one third of all Smith's recorded correspondences during Hume's lifetime; many more were lost.[30] These letters reveal that Smith and Hume felt great affection for each other, advising one another on professional, philosophic and personal matters. Smith made Hume his literary executor, and when he outlived his friend, Smith returned the favor by taking responsibility for Hume's legacy. In *WN*, Smith called Hume "by far the most illustrious philosopher and historian of the present age." (V.i.g.3) In Hume's obituary, a piece Smith wrote in the form of a letter, he spoke of his friend in the most glowing and poetic terms. He concluded by writing: "I have always considered him, both in his lifetime and since his death, as approaching as nearly the idea of a perfectly wise and virtuous man, as perhaps the nature of human frailty will permit." (*Corr.* 178)

Hume's influence on Smith is made more complex by the fact that the two disagreed more than they agreed. Yet, Smith saw himself as building upon that framework which Hume put forth, and not simply rejecting it. The core of Hume's influence is found in his doctrine of sympathy, Hume's answer to the moral sense theorists. For Hume, sympathy is a feeling of altruism that motivates human action. It is a feeling of care for humanity as a species, and represents that element of goodness, however small, that all human beings share. For Hume, sympathy is a feeling, not a capacity.

According to Hume, sympathy manifests itself as a sharing of pleasure or pain with others, where pleasure is to be understood as a feeling of approval, and pain as disapproval. Hume's theory of sympathy is analogous to his aesthetic theory in that it is naturally occurring and irrational. Since reason is concerned only with truth and falsity, moral and aesthetic judgments cannot be derived from reason. They are matters of taste and not matters of fact. This is not to say that reason plays no role. Reason may guide actions and may be used to understand moral rules once they are developed, but only sympathy can motivate an actor to abide by that which reason dictates, and only sympathy can create moral rules. Furthermore, although sympathy is naturally occurring, and the fellow-feeling of pleasure or pain that sympathy produces is a product of instinct, justice is not. The rules of justice are simply a matter of social convention and are created because they are useful. This creates an important division between moral and political theory. Traditionally, justice is regarded as being of the same character as the virtues. Hume rejects this approach, as he rejects much of the Classical Greek philosophical worldview.

Smith is in agreement with Hume regarding the importance of sympathy, but his account is much more sophisticated, as we will see. He includes an added element, the impartial spectator, as a way of making sympathy interpreted through context. Furthermore, Smith accepts the notion that moral rules are after the fact, but uses the Stoic notion of self-command to infuse reason into moral adjudication. Finally, like Hume, Smith relates justice and sympathy, but he rejects the notion that justice is either unnatural or based purely on utilitarian considerations. Smith reaffirms that justice is a virtue, although in many ways, it proves to be significantly different from the other virtues.

Hume reads Smith's theory and responds. He criticizes several points in Smith's theory, and, on one celebrated occasion, Smith explicitly adjusts his theory accordingly. In understanding Smith's philosophical development, the reader of philosophy learns something about a great philosophical friendship. One of the wonderfully exciting aspects of Smith's system, a system that makes morality dependant on the cultivation of relationships, is that by understanding the progression of Hume and Smith's friendship, we also learn more about philosophy.

3

Early and Foundational Works

Although it was customary for Scottish professors to lecture in Latin, Smith, like Hutcheson, lectured in English. He was a cautious teacher, and was worried about being misquoted. In class, he would indicate that he "hated scribblers", and thereby discouraged his students from taking notes as he lectured. This concern for accurate representation continued throughout his life, as is made evident by the many changes, both minute and substantial, that Smith ordered for each successive edition of his published work. He continued revising both *TMS* and *WN* until his death, and was always intimately involved in the process of editing for publication. Smith was concerned enough about avoiding publication of that which was not suitable, that one week before his death, he ordered sixteen volumes of his uncatalogued writing burned.

Much has been made of what might have been lost in those volumes, and scholars have expended a great deal of energy trying to reconstruct Smith's corpus. In 1930, a set of student notes was found recording Smith's lectures on rhetoric. Given Smith's predilection against allowing students to write in class, the world is lucky to have found any.

The Lectures on Rhetoric and Belles Lettres are records of lectures given at Glasgow during the years 1762 – 1763, after the first publication of *TMS* but before *WN*. In many regards, these lectures represent the best possible scenario for found notes. They are close enough to accounts of his original lectures that it is not unreasonable to assume that the content remains predominantly the same as the original lectures, but since these notes were recorded during the fifteenth winter he lectured on the topic, Smith must have had enough time to adjust and refine his arguments.

The lecture notes are useful to Smith scholars. They share common themes with both of Smith's later works, and they help shed light, not just on Smith's lecture content, but on his style as well. It was clear that Smith took rhetorical considerations very seriously, and it would be an unfortunate oversight to ignore his language and its place in his work. Ultimately, *LRBL* acts as a key for how to use language to communicate and understand Natural Philosophy, the term Smith and other Enlightenment figures used to refer to their project. To read *TMS* and *WN* without reference to *LRBL* is to exclude valuable information that sheds light on numerous unarticulated assumptions.

The lectures must be read cautiously. Smith was unaware that these student notes exited, and as a result, he could not endorse these publications. They also represent most of what Smith feared. There are numerous omissions, including the entire first lecture of the series, and the transcripts contain odd mistakes. A most obvious example is the note-taker's report that, according to Smith, "there are four things that are requisite to make a good writer", yet the transcription only records three. (i.104) There is no way of knowing whether the student erred regarding the number of criteria, whether Smith misstated them, or whether the student omitted the fourth element of the enumerated list. The interpretive principle that any reader of Smith must follow is to defer to Smith's published works whenever disagreement is identified. However, when the notes and the published works are consistent, we may regard the notes as being enlightening and reliable.

As the title indicates, Smith's lectures on rhetoric are about language use, and the proper style for different contexts. He compares, for example, the use of exclamation and authorial voice in oratory and in history, and he offers detailed discussion of argumentation and intentional manipulation in legal argument. Smith also compares specific writers, and comments on whom he regards as being a successful writer and whom he assesses as worthy of criticism. Jonathan Swift, the poet and author of political pamphlets, sermons, and, most famously, *Gulliver's Travels*, is referred to most often as the writer who has the most praiseworthy style of informative prose. Lord Shaftesbury is most often cited as the representative of great rhetorical mistakes. Smith argues that Swift's plain and direct writing style is more conducive to understanding, while Shaftesbury's very ornate style is used by the author to hide his intellectual inadequacies.

For Smith, the ultimate test for written language is not whether the author feels his or her ideas are adequately represented on paper, but, instead, whether the reader has understood correctly. Communication is successful when the two minds, that of the author and that of the reader, find some sort of meeting point; a shared understanding of the substance and emotion within the text. Smith writes:

> The accidents that befall irrational objects affect us merely their externall appearance, their Novelty, Grandeur etc. but those which affect the human Species interest us greatly by the Sympatheticall affections they raise in us. We enter into their misfortunes, grieve when they grieve, rejoice when they rejoice, and in a word feel for them in some respect as we were in the same condition. (ii.16)

\Here the reader encounters Smith's core notion *sympathy*, a term he uses to denote any fellow feeling whatsoever. It represents the unity between people, and, according to Smith, is among the most pleasing of human experiences. Smith uses sympathy to identify the moment of unity mentioned above – that shared understanding. Recall that Hume also used the notion of sympathy, but for Hume, sympathy was general and non-contextual. Here already, we see that for Smith, sympathy demands specific information for it to be successful.

Sympathy is contextual; it requires facts. As a result, it is not just poetry or polemic that seeks sympathetic understanding: it is all treatises or all styles. Take for example Smith's comments on history:

> The design of historicall writing is not merely to entertain; (this perhaps is the intention of an epic poem) besides that it has in view the instruction of the reader. It sets before us the more interesting and important events of human life, points out the causes by which these events were brought about and by this means points out to us by what manner and method we may produce similar good effects or avoid Similar bad ones. (ii.17)

Good writing is both descriptive and prescriptive. History informs its reader, not only of that which has happened, but also of that which *should* or *should not* happen again.

According to Smith, facts influence on their own. They need not be manipulated to inspire sentiments. The process of sympathy is natural; it is an inherent part of our humanity, and can be triggered without direct appeal to emotion even though it is emotion that sympathy incites. Consequently, to continue the example of the historian, the historian must present an account of events "as if he were an impartial narrator of the facts; so he uses [no] means to affect his readers,... he does not take part with either side, and for the same reason he never uses any exclamations in his own person." (i.83)

Here Smith introduces another concept that is essential to his moral and economic theories, the notion of objectivity or impartiality. Accurate moral and economic adjudication requires stepping away from one's own sentiments and adopting a position that allows for evaluating all information. In moral theory, this will be the role of the impartial spectator, a term explicitly foreshadowed in the phrase 'impartial narrator'. In economic theory, this impartiality will be found in the Smith's discussion of natural price.

There is a distinct difference between an impartial spectator and an impartial narrator. A spectator, even an active one, is outside of the action and observes phenomena from which he or she is separate. A narrator, however, is a participant, not simply because the narrator is necessarily part of the story; narrators are often spectators before or while they narrate. Narrators are participants because they choose those words that are used to convey the story. Their language choice is the major, if not sole, vehicle for sympathy. It is therefore understood by Smith that for any participant, writer or otherwise, impartiality is difficult to achieve and always limited. This notion of objectivity should not be taken so far as to suggest some Archimedean point that is free of all biases. Smith is well aware that absolute objectivity is impossible. He is not claiming that the historian should seek a 'God's eye' view, and record facts that are somehow beyond critical consideration. Instead, Smith is making a point about language use. Certain styles of writing and speech are more conducive to imparting information, and Smith is very concerned with methods of providing facts as well as ways of describing objects. (cf. i.154, and i.172-175) Perhaps this is why Smith's second lecture begins with the claim that authors should write in their own mother tongue. (i.1-2) Only in very special instances is an author able to manipulate foreign languages well enough to communicate sympathetically, because only on rare occasion is the non-native author aware of the connotations and implications inherent in language use.

Ability to construct language accurately is essential for Smith, because language plays a normative role. It is not just a medium separable from content. Language carries with it substantive claims about the message as well as the messenger. Language style must adequately represent the author. Smith illustrates this point with an unfortunate *ad hominum* against Shaftesbury in which he describes Shaftesbury's sickly childhood. According to Smith, weak constitutions are always connected to weak intellect, and Smith justifies this claim by enumerating the many failings he sees in Shaftesbury's literary and political career. (i.137-153). Any irony related to Smith's own poor health as a child is missed on Smith himself.

Nevertheless, Smith's point is important in the context of sympathy, since he seeks to show that language use, and the sentiments expressed in the language, are the primary vehicles for character identification. Smith defines the purpose of rhetoric as "the perfection of stile". (i.133) He explains that it "consists in Expressing in the most concise, proper and precise manner the thought of the author, and that in the manner which best conveys the sentiment, passion or affection with which it affects or he pretends it does affect him and which he designs to communicate to his reader." (i.133) Smith sees rhetoric as communicating sentiment, and sentiment is that which communicates a person's virtues and vices. Language use must therefore adequately represent who the author is as well as the nature of his or her character. He continues:

> For what is that makes a man agreeable company, is it not, when his sentiments appear to be naturally expressed, when the passion or affection is properly conveyed and when their thoughts are so agreeable and natural that we find ourselves inclined to give our assent to them. A wise man too in conversation and behavior will not affect a character that is unnatural to him; if he is grave he will not affect to be gay, nor if he be gay will he affect to be grave. He will only regulate his naturall temper, restrain within just bounds and lop all exuberances and bring it to that pitch which will be agreeable to those about him. But he will not affect such conduct as is unnaturall to his temper tho perhaps in the abstract they may be more to be wished. (i.135)

Smith's objection to Shaftesbury is not simply that he was a sickly child. Smith is using the biographical information as a rhetorical device to humanize an honored figure whom Smith feels may be above criticism in the minds of his students. Instead, the essence of Smith's critique is that Shaftesbury's ornate style of writing is incongruent with his "delicate temper", a phrase that Smith uses as a catch-all condemnation. (i.142) Shaftesbury's "pompous, grand and ornate" (i.145) style of writing is more suited to someone with great reasoning capacities, whereas Shaftesbury was "no great reasoner, nor deeply skilled in the abstract sciences" (i.140). Smith accuses Shaftesbury of copying Plato's style of writing as well as his theology, and as such, Smith is offended by Shaftesbury pretending to be someone whom he is not. (i.146)

This is not metaphysical gibberish on Smith's part. He is not making the absurd claim that every character type is objectively wedded to a writing style, and that Shaftesbury is somehow going against the nature of the universe by using language that he is forbidden to use. Instead, Smith is assuming a dual nature in the term 'sentiments'. It is obvious that for Smith, the term sentiment is often synonymous with the term emotion. As we saw above, he argues that the wise person must temper his or her sentiments in order to find shared sympathy. This very point is *the* topic of *TMS*. However, in the midst of his discussion of Shaftesbury, Smith explicitly defines sentiments as "moral observations", and not just as emotions. (i.144). Sentiments then, are more than just expressions of feelings; they are expressions of commitments. When a moral actor tempers his or her sentiments, the actor is tempering both emotions and moral beliefs. When a person sympathizes with someone, they are accepting, not just emotions as appropriate, but moral beliefs as well.

Writing is a vehicle for communicating sentiment in both senses of the term. Rhetoric is the study of the rules of using language towards a particular end, with a particular audience in mind. Writing is therefore a vehicle for communicating moral beliefs and rhetoric helps to prescribe the rules for transmitting those beliefs. Recall that as we saw in regards to history, writing is both descriptive and prescriptive. According to Smith, the purpose of history is not simply to report the events that have taken place, it also serves to caution the reader against doing certain things. Consequently, writing is not only morally descriptive, it is morally prescriptive as well, and when one interferes with the rules of rhetoric as Smith has accused Shaftesbury of doing – when one ignores those methods that add precision to communication – one also interferes with the ability to moralize and to educate. When Smith argues that Shaftesbury is writing against the rules of rhetoric and interfering with the accurate identification and transmission of the sentiments, he is not simply arguing that Shaftesbury is a bad writer, he is also arguing that Shaftesbury is a bad person.

It is because of the ethical role of writing and speaking that *LRBL* is filled with the language of virtue, including discussions of what language one is supposed to use when discussing virtue. For example, Smith writes: "The Language of Admiration and wonder is that in which we naturally speak of the Respectable virtues. Amplicatives and Superlatives are the terms we commonly make use of to express our admiration and respect.... Dimimutives and such-like are the terms in which we speak of objects we love." (ii.104-105) It is not, simply, that virtue makes writing better. It is that virtue makes *everything* better. Vice, by contrast, makes all things worse. Smith writes, "Virtue adds to every thing that is of itself commendable whereas Vice distracts from what would otherwise be praiseworthy." (ii.102)

In the midst of a discussion of rhetoric, Smith is immersed in ethical theory. He also discovers a potential difficulty. Sympathy is a pleasurable activity. However, if a reader sympathizes with the character in a tragedy by meeting their sentiments, would not that reader gain pleasure from the character's pain? Furthermore, which emotion does the spectator feel, the pleasure of sympathy or the pain of the actor? Smith asks and answers this question when he writes:

> We are here also to consider, that which was before hinted, that it is these uneasy emotions that chiefly affect us and give us a certain pleasing anxiety. A continued Series of Prosperity would not give near so much pleasure in the recital as an epic poem or a tragedy which make but one continued Service of unhappy Events. Even comedy itself would not give us much pleasure if we were not kept in suspense and some degree of anxiety by the cross accidents which occur and either end in or appear to threaten a misfortunate issue. For this Reason also it is not surprising that a man of an excellent heart might incline to dwell most on the dismal side of the story. (ii.11)

The subject of tragedy has been much dealt with throughout the history of philosophy and literature. Aristotle has argued in *Poetics*, for example, that tragedy is the highest form of poetry, even superior to the epic. Yet, the implication of gaining enjoyment from tragedy is that a virtuous person gains pleasure from witnessing the suffering of others. This is clearly not an understanding of virtue that many people would hold to, even if the tragedy is a fictional account of suffering. Smith begins to solve this dilemma by referring to the pleasure gained through tragedy as a "pleasing anxiety", but this seems unsatisfying because a pleasing anxiety seem to be contradictory. Smith does not resolve this issue in *LRBL*, but he does address the topic in the second addition of *TMS* when Hume brings the contradiction to his attention. We will return to this issue in the next chapter.

While reading *LRBL*, the reader is impressed by how quickly discussions of rhetoric become discussions of philosophy. Rules prescribing language-use become rules prescribing both human action and character development. Smith appears quite aware that the deeper issues cannot be resolved to anyone's satisfaction in his lectures. It becomes inevitable therefore, that Smith will do more than just discuss modes of literary presentation. The requirements of moral theory will compel Smith to spend his lifetime seeking to understand ethics. Six editions of *TMS* will result from this struggle, and, despite the popularity of WN, TMS will always remain the fulcrum of Smith's system. However, moving from *LRBL* to *TMS* would prove difficult if Smith only had his lectures to rely on. In these lectures, he offers only minimal rhetorical advice on how one should advance with argument. He does conclude his lectures with discussions of legal argumentation, but even Smith must feel that such an analysis is too narrow to be helpful in guiding the creation of a work the magnitude of *TMS*.

How does one write "didactick" texts, as Smith calls them? Smith provides two clues in *LRBL*. The first is in Lecture 24, where he suggests that one should not argue from particular to general, as Aristotle does, but, instead, looks towards Newton's method of inquiry, and argues from general to particular. Smith writes:

> In the same way in Natural Philosophy or any other Science of that Sort we may either like Aristotle go over the different branches in the order they happen to cast up to us, giving a principle commonly a new one for every phaenomenon; or in the manner of Sir Isaac Newton we may lay down certain principles known or proved in the beginning from whence we account for the several Phenomena, connecting all together by the same Chain. – This Latter we may call the Newtonian method is undoubtedly the most Philosophical, and in every science whether of Moralls or Natural philosophy etc., is vastly more ingenious and for that reason more engaging that the other. It gives us pleasure to see the phaenomena which we reckon the most unaccountable all deduced from some principle (commonly a well known one) and all united in one chain, far superior to what we feel from the unconnected method where everything is accounted for by itself without any reference to the others. (ii.134)

The second clue, found in Lecture 18, is Smith's criticism of those who leave gaps in narrative. Writing is supposed to cultivate sympathy, and sympathy is triggered by imparting information and context. When information is left incomplete, such as when a narrator leaves out part of a chronology, the reader becomes attentive to that which is left out and wonders whether there is further information that should inhibit sympathy. Smith writes: "We should never leave any chasm or Gap in the thread of the narration even tho there are no remarkable events to fill up that space. The very notion of a gap makes us uneasy for what should have happened in that time." (ii.36)

Both of these points, the method of argumentation and the avoidance of even the appearance of missing information, are references to comments made, not in *LRBL* but in an earlier essay titled *The Principles Which Lead and Direct Philosophical Enquiries; Illustrated by the History of Astronomy.*

Despite Smith's attempt to burn all his unfinished work, several fragments of a larger work survived. Smith had expressed interest in writing a "history of the liberal sciences and elegant arts", but had abandoned the plan because it was "far too extensive".[31] Among those fragments were a series of essays explaining philosophical methodology using illustrations from the history of ancient physics, the history of ancient logic and metaphysics, and, of course, the history of Astronomy. Only the latter is regarded as important by Smith scholars, but even so, *Astronomy* should be relied upon with caution. Smith was explicitly reticent about its quality. Smith had fallen ill in 1773 and had made Hume his literary executor. In a letter doing so, Smith wrote,

> As I have left the care of all my literary papers to you, I must tell you that except those which I carry along with me there are none worth the publishing, but a fragment of a great work which contains a history of Astronomical systems that were successively in fashion down to the time of Des Cartes. Whether that might not be published as a fragment of an intended juvenile work, I leave entirely to your judgment; tho I begin to suspect myself that there is more refinement than solidity in some parts of it. (*Corr.* 137)

Once again, the Smith reader must ask whether a work about which Smith himself had expressed reservations should be considered as part of his system. Smith never published *Astronomy* and he explicitly regarded it as juvenile. Nevertheless, it can be helpful. Therefore, it is important to follow the same hermeneutic principle as suggested in regards to *LRBL*. When *Astronomy* conflicts with Smith's published work, the publications should always be deferred to. However, when *Astronomy* is seen to concur with the published work, as it does quite often, it should be taken seriously as elaborations on Smith's theories.

Scholars are unsure as to when *Astronomy* was written. The best guess is some time before 1758 while he was in Edinburgh lecturing on rhetoric, but, in fact, there is enough information to suggest that he began writing it while still at Oxford as a student.[32] If this were true, he would have written *Astronomy* while he was still in his early twenties. In either case, *Astronomy* predates *TMS, WN,* and the lecture notes in *LRBL.* It is therefore useful to regard *Astronomy* as the first element of Smith's system, and, in some important way, as foundational for all that follows.

The purpose of *Astronomy* is twofold. First, it expresses human motivation to learn and do philosophy. Smith attempts to show what it is that inspires human beings to engage in inquiry, and to develop a methodology that takes such human motivation seriously. Second, *Astronomy* seeks to show why one system of thought is said to replace a previous system, and by what criteria systems should be rejected.

Not surprisingly, Smith locates the motivation for inquiry in the sentiments. Our desire to know is rooted in a series of emotions: *surprise, wonder,* and *admiration.* This is reminiscent of Aristotle's claims in *Metaphysics.*[33] That which is unexpected brings about surprise, that which is expected brings about wonder, and that which is great or beautiful brings about admiration. (intro.1) Yet, the three sentiments do not act alone; they act in concert. Smith writes "these sentiments, like all others when inspired by one and the same object, mutually support and enliven one another." (intro.6)

Surprise, wonder, and admiration form a chain and a sense of closure to many events. Upon discovering an unknown or unexpected piece of information, the observer – spectator in Smith's language – feels anxiety that Smith equates to "panic terrors". (I.4) He or she wonders about the place this new event holds in our universe and organizes it into a scheme of understanding, perhaps creating a new system in the process. Only then can the spectator admire the beauty of the new or revised system, and the spectator does so in much the same manner that one admires an elegant machine, an equation, or a work of art.

The natural desire to form a system, a human quality that Smith will make much of in *TMS* and in *WN,* forces one to seek explanatory principles that sufficiently unite phenomena. Smith writes:

> It is evident that the mind takes pleasure in observing the resemblances that are discoverable betwixt different objects. It is

30

by means of such observations that it endeavours to arrange and methodise all its ideas, and to reduce them into proper classes and assortments. Where it can observe but one single quality, that is common to a great variety of otherwise widely different objects, that single circumstance will be sufficient for it to connect them together, to reduce them to one common class, and to call them by one general name. (II.2)

For Smith, the inability to categorize novel events is analogous to the to lack of information that is a barrier to sympathy in narration. Incomplete information creates a gap that makes a spectator unsatisfied with his or her worldview. There is reason to believe that Smith derives this notion from Hume's conception of causation in *A Treatise of Human Nature*. In his *Treatise*, Hume argues that relation is visible only in effects, and that senses cannot prove that which is commonly called causation. Instead, an event is said to cause another when the two are expected to appear in repeated sequence. They are thus artificially regarded as having some connection other than the sequence of time.[34]

Smith has similar notions. He writes:

When objects succeed each other in the same train in which the ideas of the imagination have been thus accustomed to mover, and in which, though not conducted by that chain of events presented to the senses, they have acquired a tendency to go on of their own accord, such objects appear all closely connected with one another, and the thought glides easily along with them, without effort and without interruption. (II.8)

According to Smith, sentiments originate in the imagination. It is also the imagination where Smith locates what other philosophers have called the understanding. For Smith, then, the imagination easily follows any chain of events. However, when a chain is broken, the spectator is stricken by surprise, and seeks to recreate the chain, perhaps with different elements.

Here, Smith deepens the connection between *Astronomy* and *LRBL*. A gap in a narrative interferes with the listener's sympathetic union with the narrator. The analogous is true of didactic prose. In *Astronomy*, Smith writes:

But if this customary connection be interrupted, if one or more objects appear in an order quite different from that to which the imagination has been accustomed, and for which it is prepared,... we are at first surprised by the unexpectedness of the new appearance, and when the momentary emotion is over, we still wonder how it came to occur in that place. The imagination no longer feels the usual facility of passing from the event which goes before to that which comes after. (II.8)

The presence of a gap in a scientific theory, like the presence of a gap in narrative, causes suspicion and unease. The moment a satisfying explanation is offered, the unease "vanishes altogether." (II.9) As Smith himself asks, "who wonders at the machinery of the opera-house who has once been admitted behind the scenes?" (II.9)

The desire to know is caused by the sentiments, and philosophy is that process by which an inquirer seeks to resolve unpleasant emotions. In this regard, Smith had foreshadowed Charles S. Peirce's 1877 publication, *The Fixation of Belief,* in which Peirce argues that answers are only acceptable when they permanently quell unease, and that such a standard is sufficient to reject any but the most scientific of methods.[35]

Smith sees inquiry as an investigation of a chain of thought, and philosophy guides inquiry. In *Astronomy*, Smith defines philosophy as "the science of the connecting principles of nature". (II.12) Accordingly, Smith indicates that a philosopher is motivated to create systems because his or her mind is more finely tuned to the gaps in the chain of events. The philosopher sees missing information where others do not. He writes:

Philosophy, by representing the invisible chains which bind together all these disjointed objects endeavours to introduce order into this chaos of jarring and discordant appearances, to allay this tumult of the imagination, and to restore it, when it surveys the great revolutions of the universe, to the tone of tranquility and composure, which is both most agreeable in itself, and most suitable to its nature. (II.12)

For Smith, philosophy is a natural enterprise. It is the result of anxieties that are themselves part of what it means to be human. It is the product of fear, and is as inevitable as the sentiments upon which it is based.

Since *Astronomy* is an historical essay, Smith moves from his definition of philosophy to an account of its origin. Smith is an Enlightenment figure. As discussed in chapter one, a major goal of the

Enlightenment was to challenge the prevailing religious worldview and to replace, whenever possible, theological explanations with general explanatory principles. Smith does this in *Astronomy* by pointing out that primitive ignorance resulted in constant fear but that, over time, the beauty of nature divided events into that which is fearful and that which is not. As before, Smith focuses on novelty and irregularity, and its effect on the sentiments. In doing so, Smith introduces his most famous metaphor, 'the invisible hand', a phrase that, despite its notoriety, occurs only three times in all of Smith's corpus, once in *TMS*, once in *WN,* and once in the following passage of *Astronomy*:

> It is the irregular events of nature only that are ascribed to the agency of their gods. Fire burns, and water refreshes; heavy bodies descend, and lighter substances fly upwards by the necessity of their own nature; now was the invisible hand of Jupiter ever apprehended to be employed in these matters. But thunder and lightening, storms and sunshine, those more irregular events were ascribed to his favour or his anger. (III.2)

The purpose of the phrase "the invisible hand" is to highlight the projection of intelligence where there is none, or, at least, where there is none perceived. Notice, that the polytheistic religions of which Smith speaks in this passage attribute natural events to the invisible hand of Jupiter. Smith also explains that the religions ascribe these events to the worthiness of the religious adherents:

> With him [the religious believer], therefore, every object of nature, which is by its beauty or greatness, and whose operations are not perfectly regular, is supposed to act by the direction of some invisible and designing power. The sea is spread out into a calm, or heaved into a storm, according to the good pleasure of Neptune. Does the earth pour forth an exuberant harvest? It is owing to the indulgence of Ceres. Does the vine yield a plentiful vintage? It flows from the bounty of Bacchus. Do either refuse their presents? It is ascribed to the displeasure of those offended deities. (III.2)

In this context, the invisible hand is a fiction. It is an explanation designed to soothe fear and anxiety, it is the product of wonder about the universe, and a means of explanation. Upon its acceptance, those who believe its power admire its beauty and greatness. Although the invisible hand is a remnant of an ancient system – one that has long been surpassed – the metaphor has enough power over a more "civilized" time, that it is the key element that the contemporary world remembers most of Adam Smith's philosophy. How the metaphor is to be understood economically is addressed in chapters three and four.

For *Astronomy*, there remains one more problem, and its details constitute the vast majority of the essay. If the invisible hand is the remnant of an obsolete system, what motivated the rejection of that system? What is it that makes one system superior over another? Why have human beings chosen to reject polytheism in favor of monotheism and why have Enlightenment philosophers chosen to reject monotheism in favor of scientific method? Finally, why has Newton replaced Aristotle, as Smith acknowledges in *LRBL?*

For Smith, the ultimate criteria for believability must always be the sentiments. Smith's essay enumerates numerous systems of astronomy, and in doing so he shows how, viewed over time, systems become more intricate. The paradigmatic example of complexity in astronomy will always be the epicycle, the spiral circular motion ascribed to planets that were said to complement their orbits. Epicycles were used by Ptolemy to add precision to his predictions, but even with their existence, much of the mathematics was approximate at best. Such theories ceased to be believable, because their complexity inhibited their greatness, and their unpredictability always elicited surprise. This gave way to wonder and anxiety. Smith writes:

> This system had now become so intricate and complex as those appearances themselves, which it had been invented to render uniform and coherent. The imagination, therefore, found itself but little relieved from that embarrassment, into which those appearances had thrown it, by so perplexed an account of things. (IV.8)

The Ptolemaic system, itself the replacement for earlier astronomical systems, gives way to Copernicus' system. Copernicus' theory was revised by Galileo and Kepler, and was eventually replaced by Descartes' work, which itself was replaced by Newton's. It is now well known, of course, that Newtonian physics has been surpassed by Einstein's theory of relativity, and of course, most theorists understand the likelihood of science progressing ever further.

Two points can be ascertained from Smith's detailed history. First, according to Smith, as systems advance, complexity decreases. In a passage that betrays Smith's commitment to the Enlightenment mechanistic worldview, Smith indicates:

Systems in many respects resemble machines. A machine is a little system created to perform as well as to connect together, in reality, those different movements and effects which the artist has occasion for. A system is an imaginary machine invented to connect together in the fancy of those different movements and effects which are already in reality performed. The machines that are first invented to perform any particular movement are always the most complex, and succeeding artists generally discover that, with fewer wheels, with fewer principles of motion, than had originally been employed, the same effects may be easily produced. The first systems, in the same manner, are always the most complex, and a particular connecting chain, or principle, is generally thought necessary to unite every two seemingly disjointed appearance: but it often happens that one great connecting principle is afterwards found to be sufficient to bind together all the discordant phaenomena that occur us a whole species of things. (IV.19)

Systems become rejected because they become too complex. Complexity is the product of too many laws, and the lack of one unifying principle. Thus, we see why, in *LRBL*, Smith rejected Aristotle's approach of moving from the particular to the general in favor of Newton's method of theorizing from the general to the particular. Aristotle's theory is not simple enough. By beginning with individual principles, one begins with a multiplicity, but multiplicities are that which should be avoided because they inspire surprise and wonder. According to Smith, Aristotle's process is inefficient and leads to anxiety. We also see why, in *LRBL*, Smith rejects Shaftesbury as being too ornate. Ornate writing has superfluities. Shaftesbury's literary flourishes are analogous to astronomical epicycles. If Swift can write more simply and sympathize more effectively than Shaftesbury can, then clearly Swift's work is superior. One sees direct parallels between patterns of human psychology and the operations of the physical world. Swift is Newton to Shaftesbury's Aristotle.

The second point involves the meaning of impartiality. Recall that in historical writing, as well as the didactic form, the author must act as an impartial narrator. I have already argued that Smith does not mean to equate impartiality with absolute objectivity, some Archimedean standpoint, or an impossible-to-achieve God's eye-view. Ultimately, what is lost when one gives up objectivity of this sort is any claim to absolute certainty. Impartiality is the key to good judgment, but it is not

35

the key to infallibility. If *Astronomy* teaches us anything at all, it is that scientific theories are not timeless. Despite Smith's faith in Newtonian astronomy – Smith has enough faith in Newton's system that he, quite polemically, argues that one would "look in vain" for a more advanced system (IV.76) – he is at root a skeptic about certainty. Perhaps he is optimistic in his skepticism in that he believes in the possibility of some sort of impartiality, but he is still skeptical enough to understand that impartiality has its limits. Skepticism is a form of impartiality because it recognizes the possibility of fallibility and compels the wise to question their own conclusions.

Smith continues to makes much of the human desire for systems throughout his career. He continually associates it with the imagination, and in *WN*, he attributes to it great political harm. For Smith, in the political arena, the human love of system can only be balanced by a limited government. Its effects can be dispelled, at least in part, by adherence to the doctrine of the invisible hand. Ironically, and quite consciously, Smith understands that the doctrine of the invisible hand, although a remedy for the love of system, is itself an element of a system and can be used to soothe the anxieties and the surprises caused by novelty and irregular events. One admires the invisible hand as much as one admires anything.

Smith's early work defines the problematic that he will continue to work within. The rules of rhetoric and the philosophical method operate in unison to create a linguistic and argumentative structure that is informative about the subject matter, about the author, and about the reader as well. Through these two early works, Smith shows his readers that inquiry is as much about the inquirer as it is about the subject matter investigated. Philosophy is the product of sentiments, and sentiments play dual roles. They are emotions that inspire us and they are moral commitments that guide us. To separate the two is to deny what it means to be human. We are seekers in a community of seekers. A fundamental goal of human life is to ask, not just what it means to seek, but what it means to seek *together*.

Smith's next move is clear. He must investigate the connection between our emotions and the rules that govern their propriety. For Smith to advance, he must not limit his inquiry to the descriptive role played by the emotions – that information which our emotions report to others through their expression – he must also inquire into the prescriptive role of our emotions by investigating those criteria that will direct our commitments. Smith must offer his readers, not simply a theory of any sentiments. He must offer his readers a theory of *moral* sentiments.

4

The Theory of Moral Sentiments

The first edition of *The Theory of Moral Sentiments* was published in 1759 while Smith was Chair of Logic at the University of Glasgow. It is believed that much of the text follows Smith's lectures on ethics, and the rhetorical style bears this out. The book is written as a teacher would write. It is entertaining, and motivating. It assumes an interested but not fully informed audience. The writing is designed to pull the reader into the text as a teacher would pull a student into a lecture, and to do so, Smith uses vivid examples, plain language, and subtle direction.

Perhaps the most striking feature of the book is the narrative writing style that borders on conversation. It is a personal book, and is made so, at least in part, by the use of what Charles L. Griswold Jr. calls the 'protreptic' *we*, in other words, the use of a rhetorically directing pronoun. [36] Smith uses the *we* to enforce a kind of camaraderie between the author and the reader. *We* feel emotion at the misery of others. (I.i.1.1) *We* are affected by heroism. (I.iii.1.14) *We* examine our own passions in the light of the passions of others. (III.1.5) In making the relationship between author and reader explicit, Smith encourages the reader to both recognize his or her own pre-philosophical emotional commitments, and his or her role in the community of which the author is also a part.

Smith is not ornate in his writing. In that regard, he follows the example of Swift and learns from Shaftesbury's mistakes. Furthermore, *TMS* follows the Newtonian "didactick" style as outlined in *LRBL*. It begins with a general principle and detail if offered only after it's main claim has been established. Smith's opening words are both a commitment to and an attack on a particular principle. Smith writes

> How selfish soever man may be supposed, there are evidently some principles in his nature, which interest him in the fortune of others, and render their happiness necessary to him, though he derives nothing from it except the pleasure of seeing it. (I.i.1.1)

Most important, the opening sentence of *TMS* is an attack on the ethical theories of Thomas Hobbes and Bernard Mandeville. In *Leviathan* (1651), Hobbes argues that humans are ultimately selfish. They act out of animalistic needs, and when unfettered by rules of government, they are motivated without any concern for others. The state of nature – that period before the formation of a government – is a state of fear. Political organization is formed out of the necessity of reducing the harshness of life. The sovereign, that person or group who governs by the consent of the parties in the social contract and whose purpose it is to enforce the social contract's terms, frightens or forces citizens into obedience, and only in such a situation will people respect the civil rights of others. Only 'civil' rights are respected in Hobbes's state because, according to Hobbes, the natural right – the right to everything – is relinquished in exchange for the security of the state.

Hobbes is a relativist. His ethical theories rely heavily on the his linguistic analysis, and language is purely subjective. Good is defined as that which an individual loves and desires. Evil is defined as that which an individual hates and is averse to. He is also mechanistic. He extends Descartes' claim that animals are machines to a general claim about human beings: humans are machines and freedom is defined simply as the unfettered movement of limbs. The consequence of his claims is an all-powerful sovereign, a view of the human animal as fundamentally selfish, and a rejection of the normative power of virtue theory. Virtue theory is that system of ethics that defines morality in terms of the Greek conception of *areté*, which translates as either human excellence or virtue.

Bernard Mandeville, like Smith, was an economist as well as an ethicist. His book, *The Fable of the Bees,* was first published in 1705 as a poem titled *The Grumbling Hive: or, Knaves Turn's Honest.* Twenty-four years later, the volume was completed as a collection of responses to popular and philosophical criticisms of the poem. In his work,

Mandeville argues that the manufacture of necessities do not create enough wealth to drive a national economy, and that moral theory should be reconceived to value the requisite luxuries that had been denied by a puritan asceticism. Luxuries should be manufactured and consumption should be encouraged to the most excessive degree. According to Mandeville, the encouragement of vice benefits society as a whole. Envy, vanity and other such sentiments result in excessive spending, which in turn bring employment and wealth. He claims that such vices should be encouraged because vice encourages trade. Even crime keeps locksmiths and police employed. Mandeville's theory is easily reduced to the slogan that is the alternative title of his work: "Private Vices; Publick Benefits".

Mandeville rejects moralistic responses along the line of Shaftesbury's argument that people are ultimately benevolent. Shaftesbury's claims inspires Mandeville's somewhat sarcastic response, "What pity it is that they are not true?" [37] He writes:

> That boasted middle way, and the calm Virtues recommended in the Characteristicks [Shaftesbury's great work], are good for nothing but to breed Drones, and might qualify a Man for the stupid Enjoyments of a Monastick Life, or at best a Country Justice of Peace, but they would never fit him for Labour and Assiduity, or stir him up to great Atchievements and perilous Undertakings. Man's natural love of Ease and Idleness, and Proneness to indulge in sensual Pleasures, are not to be cured by Precept: His strong Habits and Inclinations can only be subdued by Passion of greater Violence.[38]

Both Hobbes and Mandeville argue that humans are selfish by nature and that one cares for others only insofar as it benefits oneself. In the first sentence of *TMS*, Smith is countering this claim. We may be *supposed* to be selfish, Smith argues, but there are *evidently* some principles that provide spectators with pleasure at seeing the happiness of others. Notice the rhetorical association of *supposition* with Hobbes and Mandeville's claim of selfishness, and the association of *evidence* with Smith's assertion of the possibility of altruism. Already in the first sentence, Smith is associating his own work with the science of Newton, and the scientific and empirical method. Smith adds to his attack by invoking the protreptic we in the next sentence. He writes, "Of this kind is pity or compassion, the emotion which we feel for the misery of others, when we either see it, or are made to conceive it in a very lively manner." (I.i.1.1) Incited by the use of *we*, the reader reflects and finds that he or she does indeed feel pity or compassion when confronted with the misery of others, and such an acknowledgment is enough to postpone an explicit attack on Mandeville and Hobbes until a much later section of *TMS*.

Also in the first two sentences of *TMS*, Smith introduces the notion that responsive sentiments – sentiments that are inspired by others – are to be understood as a outgrowth of an individual's role as spectator. Smith's operating metaphor throughout *TMS* is that of theater. Humans watch others, and, eventually, watch themselves as if through the eyes of others. It is thus that moral judgments are developed, and it is only through this process of seeing and being seen that virtue is cultivated.

The Theory of Moral Sentiments is primarily a book about identity. It is, among other things, an exercise in understanding the nature of a relational self. In many ways, *TMS* is communitarian, not liberal, where communitarian is understood as acknowledging some priority of the community and liberal is understood as a commitment to the priority of the individual.[39] Smith writes:

> Were it possible that a human creature could grow up to manhood in some solitary place, without any communication with his own species, he could no more think of his own character, of the propriety or demerit of his own sentiments and conduct, of the beauty or deformity of his own mind, then the beauty and deformity of his own face . . .. (III.I.3-5)

Smith's communitarian nature is seen most effectively in his discussion of *sympathy*, Smith's term for the mechanism that allows people to observe and adopt the fellow-feeling which corresponds to "any-passion whatever" that is observed in others. (I.i.I.5) We have already encountered sympathy as that moment of unity between author and reader in *LRBL*, and in Smith's rhetorical claims in both *LRBL* and *Astronomy*, that writing should avoid gaps in chronology or argumentative chain to order to avoid causing anxiety over missed information. The use of sympathy in *TMS* is in direct concordance with its use in earlier works.

Sympathy is not compassion as it is normally understood, nor is it the generalized and non-contextual love of humanity that Hume describes. Sympathy is a compelling force that attempts to translate all human emotions from one person to another. It allows one person, the spectator, to understand the emotions of a second person, the actor. It also forms the foundation of moral judgment by devising criteria of acceptable action.

Using sympathy, moral standards are constructed in three ways. First, the use of sympathy allows spectators to approve or disapprove of the actions of others by testing whether they would act similarly in similar situations. Second, the use of sympathy provides a mechanism for the actor's evaluation of the spectator's judgments. Through sympathy, the actor can assess the judgments of spectators to determine whether the spectators think the action is appropriate. Third, the use of sympathy affords the actor with the capacity to create an imagined impartial spectator who (a) provides the foundation for determining whether the judgments of the real spectators are worthy of abiding by, and (b) provides the foundation for determining the morality of actions when no other spectators are actually present. Thus sympathy does not simply identify those acts that are to be praised, it identifies those acts that are praiseworthy. For Smith, the impartial spectator is a theory of conscience. Recall the origins of the impartial spectator in *LRBL* where Smith argues that in historical prose the authorial voice must act as an impartial narrator.

The mechanism of sympathy works as follows: through sympathy, a spectator observes the actions or emotions of others. In this context, actions and emotions can be regarded as analogous because of the dual nature of the term "sentiments". As previously discussed, for Smith, sentiments mean both emotion and moral commitment. Given the outward and observable signals from the actor, the spectator imagines what he or she perceives the actor's emotion to be and, by using the imagination, creates his or her own less-perfect and less intense version of it. If sympathy is possible – if the spectator can adopt the sentiment of the actor – then the actor's action is deemed as appropriate by the spectator. If sympathy is impossible – if the spectator finds it impossible to adopt the sentiment of the actor – then the spectator regards the act as worthy of condemnation. Being a spectator is thus an active role. It is indicative of Smith's shared faith with the ancients that theater is participatory enough that it can be a primary vehicle for moral education. Aristotle, for example, would not have engaged in his discussion of tragedy in *Poetics* if the audience member were seen simply as a passive receptacle. The spectator has an intimate reactive relationship with the actor.

At this point, Smith must come to terms with Hume's criticism. Recall the problem with tragedy is that the characters suffer, yet the audience gains a pleasing anxiety from watching them, and that such an emotion seems contradictory. Hume expresses this in a letter to Smith:

I wish you had more particularly and fully prov'd, that all kinds of Sympathy are necessarily Agreeable. This is the Hinge of your system, and yet you only mention the matter cursorily in p. 20. Now it would appear that there is a disagreeable Sympathy, as well as an agreeable:... It is always thought a difficult Problem to account for the Pleasure received from the Tears and Grief and Sympathy of Tragedy; which would not be the Case, if all Sympathy was agreeable. An Hospital would be a more entertaining Place than a Ball. I am afraid that in p. 99 and 111 this Proposition has escaped you, or rather is interwove with your Reasonings in that place. You say expressly, *it is painful to go along with Grief and we always enter into it with Reluctance*. It will probably be requisite for you to modify or explain this Sentiment, and reconcile it to your System. (*Corr.* 36)

Hume's argument that all sympathy cannot be agreeable if an actor is reluctant to enter into grief of another is an important one, and Smith addresses it in a footnote inserted in the second edition. Attached to Hume's cited sentence, "But it is painful to go along with grief and we always enter into it with reluctance" (I.iii.1.9), Smith writes:

It has been objected to me that as I found the sentiment of approbation, which is always agreeable, upon sympathy, it is inconsistent with my system to admit any disagreeable sympathy. I answer, that in the sentiment of approbation there are two things to be taken notice of; first the sympathetic passion of the spectator; and, secondly, the emotion which arises from his observing the perfect coincidence between this sympathetic passion in himself, and the original passion in the person principally concerned. This last emotion, in which the sentiment of approbation properly consists, is always agreeable and delightful. The other may either be agreeable or disagreeable, according to the nature of the original passion, whose feature it must always, in some measure, retain. (I.iii.1.9.note)

Smith's answer to Hume is a further example of the complexity added by Smith to Hume's use of sympathy. Smith introduces a second order emotion that observes the concordance of the actor's original emotion and the sympathetic emotion of the spectator. When the spectator sympathizes with the actor, he or she feels whatever emotion the actor feels, whether it be pleasurable or painful. But, upon meeting the sentiment, the spectator feels an *additional* sentiment, that of the pleasure of unity or community. It is similar to the joy one feels, not when a friend is in grief, but from the intimacy that results in assisting friends with grief. It is also similar to the joy felt in unified commiseration when one finds another person who has shared similar traumatic experiences. It is, in some sense, similar to discovering one is not alone. No joy is felt with the knowledge that others have suffered, only that there is someone with whom to share complex emotions. The two are intimately connected and difficult to distinguish. In an early version of his reply to Hume, Smith included an acknowledgement of the difficulty in identifying the two discrete emotions. Smith included the following sentence in editions 2-5 but rejected it in the sixth edition that is now regarded as definitive: "Two sounds, I suppose, may each of them taken singly, be austere, and yet, if they are perfectly concords, the perception of their harmony and coincidence may be agreeable." (*Corr.* 40) Smith is not explicit as to why he chose to remove it.

Context is essential in identifying the cause of either of the sentiments. One must be aware of as many facts as possible. This is true both in order to understand which emotion originates where, and in order to have an eye for all relevant facts. Attention to detail in this regard is crucial because, according to Smith, the spectator looks at the cause and context of the agent's emotions more than the emotions themselves. Smith writes:

Sympathy, therefore, does not arise so much from the view of the passion, as from that of the situation which excites it. We sometimes feel for another, a passion of which he himself seems to be altogether incapable; because, when we put ourselves in his case, that passion arises in our breast from the imagination, though it does not in his reality. (I.i.1.10)

This is an essential point for Smith. If the spectator were just making a determination based on the observation of a particular emotion, hermeneutics would not be a problem. Although there would be room for empirical failure, mistakes such as confusing anger with excitement might be rare, and should such mistakes occur, they would be easily overcome by either extending the conversation or the period of observation. Instead, according to Smith, the spectator is making a judgment based upon the facts of the case. What happened to the actor that caused him or her to hold certain sentiments is ultimately more important than the emotion that the person appears to be expressing. The spectator must therefore be aware of as many details as possible, extending as far back in time as one is able, as well as be aware of any possible consequences not yet experienced. This too is reminiscent of Smith's discussion in *LRBL* in which Smith argues that facts in and of themselves have the power to cultivate sympathy independent of polemic manipulation.

Yet, sympathy is both contextual and perspectival. It respects the differences between people, and Smith's explanations acknowledge that who one is will greatly influence how one feels. Sympathy does not require that the spectator simply put him or herself in the situation of another person, it asks the spectator to determine the appropriate sentiments based on how, given the facts of the agents life, this *particular* agent should act in this *particular* situation. As Smith writes:

> When I condole with you for the loss of your only son, in order to enter into your grief I do not consider what I, a person of such a character and profession, should suffer, if I had a son, and if that son was unfortunately to die: but I consider what I should suffer if I was really you, and I not only change circumstances with you, but I change persons and characters. My grief, therefore, is entirely upon your account, and not in the least upon my own. (VII.iii.1.4)

To determine the cause, the context, and the possible ends of any situation, the spectator must also understand the actor. He or she must investigate the actor's reactions to other similar situations and to the consequences that resulted from them. Familiarity then, joins attentiveness as necessary conditions for sympathy. The farther removed the spectator is from the agent, the more difficult a true understanding of the situation and the agent becomes. Self-knowledge is also crucial to spectator attentiveness. A spectator must learn to be aware of his or her own limitations, and of his or her own ignorance. For Smith, the more knowledge any person has, the more capacity they have to sympathize.

Smith argues that human beings, by nature, are endowed with:

> an original desire to please, and an original aversion to offend his brethren. She taught him to feel leisure in their favourable, and pain in their unfavourable regard. She rendered their approbation most flattering and most agreeable to him for its own sake; and their disapprobation most mortifying and most offensive. (III.2.6)

Smith argues that human beings *want* to sympathize with others and will act in accordance with those norms that society deems appropriate because they hope to enjoy the pleasure of mutual sympathy. According to Smith, humans, by nature, are hard-wired to not only respond to negative or positive reinforcement, but to struggle to anticipate social judgments in advance. A properly socialized actor will judge his or her own actions as an attempt to govern, in the place of society, his or her own actions. The actor imagines that he or she is the spectator and is impartially watching someone else act even though the action is the actor's own. Furthermore, on those occasions where the agent feels compelled to disagree with society's judgment, it is the impartial spectator's judgment that forms the foundation of conscience. Since the impartial spectator has a history of being reliable, the agent may defer to the judgment of the impartial spectator in cases of conflict.

We see here, the possibility of disagreement between individual and society, and its connection to the imagination. Sympathy is only possible because of this capacity. The human endowment with imagination highlights an important tension within Smith's appraisal of the human condition: the fundamentally discrete nature of human perception. He writes: "As we have no immediate experience of what other men feel, we can form no idea of the manner in which they are affected, but by conceiving what we ourselves should feel in the like situation." (I.i.I.2) In other words, individuals can never know with any certainty what it is other people feel. Individuals must therefore rely on their imagination and their own experiences regarding the emotion in question to inform them of the sensations of others.

Smith uses the imagination to overcome the difficulties that are generally associated with the problem of other minds. According to Smith, we cannot access direct or privileged experience of others. We can only imagine what the experiences of others might be based upon observable signs and based upon our own experiences. For Smith, sympathy is, in part, the repeated act of gaining more and more information in order to be better informed as to what the sentiments of an agent are and ought to be.

Imagination does not necessarily accurately inform spectators of another's sensations since it is based on the spectator's own experiences and not the actors. Smith writes: "It is the impressions of our own sense only, not those of his [the person being observed], which our imaginations copy." Smith continues:

> By the imagination we place ourselves in his situation, we conceive ourselves enduring all of the same torments, we enter as it were into his body, and become in some measure the same

person with him and thence form some idea of his sensations, and even feel something which, though weaker in degree, is not altogether unlike them ... so to conceive or to imagine that we are in it, excites some degree of the same emotion, in proportion to the vivacity or dullness of the conception. (I.i.I.2)

Notice Smith's language. The above quote highlights that through the imagination spectators only *conceive* themselves as enduring the same passions as the agents they observe. The spectator enters *as it were* into the body of the agent. For the most part, Smith's language is filled with qualifiers that are meant to inspire doubt regarding how much one can know about the sentiments of others.

For Smith, to have immediate or direct knowledge of the sentiments of another person is an epistemological impossibility. A person can only base comparison on those sentiments to which they themselves have direct access. As a result, the sentiments that are created through the imagination are not determined by the sentiments of others. Instead, they are based on the sentiments of the person who imagines them; he or she infers them to be equivalent sentiments to those of the person being observed. Any determination of sentiments is an inference based upon the observable effects of the sentiments and does not constitute definitive or direct knowledge of the causes themselves. Although Smith's description of sympathy may seem to imply that an emotion is transferred from one person to another, this is not the case. A spectator determines the actor's sentiments through observation and by the process of falsification; sympathy is a product of the imagination. Cultivation of sympathy is the most accurate when the spectator is conscious of the possibility of mistakes. Sympathy is subject to falsification in that inappropriate moral judgments are corrected by the community in conjunction with the moral actor him or herself.

For Smith, human beings are, in at least one important way, fundamentally separate from one another. We are divided into spectator and actor and, according to Smith, we know only our own sensations. For Smith, to know others' sentiments is to understand how observable data are to be interpreted through sympathy and to accept the ability of the community and the impartial spectator to point out mistakes. He places great weight on emphasizing how inaccurate imagination is and how education is necessary to help remedy the imperfections of the imagination and of sympathy. In this context, education should be understood in its widest sense – that information can be learned through both formal and informal means.

46

Imagination is the bridge that creates community and it is enabled through education. Moral judgment is a product of interaction, and is enabled by the ability to learn about others. Thinking for oneself is a group activity. It allows an individual to be constituted at least in part by others, even if persons are, at root, fundamentally separate. It also allows moral agents to use standards of dignity and personhood as criteria for determining how to treat others. Take, for example, Smith's discussion of slavery.

Smith condemns slavery in numerous ways, some of which are economic. However, for Smith, the most powerful condemnation is that condemnation based upon morality. He could not be stronger than when he writes: "There is not a Negro from the coast of Africa who does not, in this respect, possess a degree of magnanimity which the soul of his sordid master is too often scarce capable of conceiving. Fortune never exerted more cruelly her empire over mankind, than when she subjected those nations of heroes to the refuse of the jails of Europe." (V.2.9) The slave owner, according to Smith, is much too far removed from the day to day life of a slave to sympathize of his or her own accord with the emotions felt by the slave, and any attempt to sympathize would only lead towards pain and self-condemnation by the slave owner. How can a person possibly approve of the pain of oppression if they themselves are the oppressor? Would that not involve hating oneself? This would seem necessarily so, especially since, as Smith writes "when we see one man oppressed or injured by another, the sympathy which we feel with the distress of the sufferer seems to serve only to animate our fellow feelings with his resentment against the offender." (II.i.2.4)

Smith claims that if suffering is unjustly caused, any fellow feeling towards those who are suffering will naturally result in disapproval of the cause of the suffering. The slave owner is the person causing the suffering. By sympathizing with the slave, the slave owner adopts the sentiments of the slave including the profound animosity the slave feels for her or his oppressor. Sympathizing would then be the process of the slave owner adopting the attitude of the slave, the necessary consequence of which would be self-hatred. The slave owner would feel that animosity towards him or herself.[40]

Smith acknowledges the darker side of human nature. For example, he admits that people have a natural love of dominance over others. (*WN* III.ii.10) However, this love of dominance, and its consequent slavery, can be curbed through sympathy and through education, although Smith does acknowledge that this may take the passage of many generations and the strongest government intervention.[41] American history certainly bears this out.

Time and education contribute to social change and the awareness of the civil rights of others. However, there are always those who cannot be affected by social change, or who are indifferent to the pleas of society. About them, Smith can only raise his hands in exasperation. Griswold most eloquently writes:

> If a slave owner were insensible to all appeals of humanity, uncomprehending of demonstrations of his errors about the alleged utility of the system, and indifferent to the reduction of justice to the exercise of brute force, then he would fall outside the sphere of ethical conversation. In such a case, neither Smith's nor anyone else's arguments will reach him. If there is truth to the "intuitionism" or "immediacy" view of moral "perception," it is here. Imagine that after going through all of the considerations just described, an "indifferent spectator" is presented with the spectacle of husband and wife and children being violently and permanently separated and sold into slavery. Imagine that this spectator is truly "indifferent," feeling nothing, and is still unable to understand why this horrible event merits his condemnation. Here we would declare: "He just doesn't see it," and discussion would come to an end.[42]

The indifferent spectator is condemned because he or she is unable to *care* for others, and in Smith's system, if close proximity, education, and social pressure cannot influence a spectator to see the humanity of an agent, there is no recourse but that of law and government intervention. If the lawmakers are themselves slave owners, then, as Smith writes elsewhere, there is little chance that slavery would ever be abolished until the subjects of the regime rebel. (LJ (A) iii.116-117)

Given the example of slavery, we can see a striking difference between Smith's moral system and more contemporary liberal essentialist systems such as John Rawls' *A Theory of Justice*,[43] published in 1971. It sought to reconcile social contract theory with Kant's arguments for the normative value of objective rational deliberation. These two elements are most intimately connected in Rawls' original position, a device of representation that serves as both a substitute for the state of nature and Kant's context-independent categorical imperative. Students of Rawls will recall that in the original position, individuals are under a veil of ignorance, a mechanism that provides selective ignorance. This veil shields all participants from information regarding their own social status and capabilities. Individuals in the original position are mutually self-interested, and will choose only those principles that will result in those institutions that benefit them, as individuals.[44] The normativity and persuasiveness of *A Theory of Justice* lie in Rawls' claim that *all* individuals so situated will *always* choose the same principles of justice.

Deliberation in the original position leads to the formation of society. The nature of political institutions is developed based upon Rawls' *maximin* principle. This principle states that given a list of options regarding the structure of the state, agents in the original position will choose those institutions in which the least well-off in one society are in a better situation as compared to the least well-off individuals in all other possible societies. In other words, agents will choose that option which results in the maximum amount of good for those people who are in the minimum social position, hence the term *maximin*.[45] Since the agents determining the principles of justice do not know their place in society, they must assume that it is likely that they will end up part of the worst-off group in society. Rawls even suggests that agents should assume that their enemies will determine their place in society, thereby guaranteeing that agents will always find themselves in the lowest rung. Consequently, according to Rawls, agents will necessarily choose institutions in which the lowest rung is the most beneficial of all possible lowest rungs and that economic inequality is permissible insofar as the inequality contributes to the increased well being of the least fortunate.

According to Rawls, human beings do not like to gamble. Moral and political adjudication is reasoning about *safe* options. One would never choose a society in which he or she would not be guaranteed the best possible minimal condition. Moral thinking is economic. Given several options, one will always choose the choice with the greatest level of immediate satisfaction as opposed to risk or potential, regardless of the odds. Notice that the justification for Rawls' principles of justice is that the worst-case scenario might happen to the deliberating subject and that people chose liberal democracy out of fear. Rawls does not claim, as Smith would, that the justification for the principles of justice are simply that treating people one way as opposed to another is inherently wrong. Whereas for Smith, the connection between agent and spectator is a relationship of consideration, the agents in the original position, by design, do not care about others.

Compare also the mutually self-interested Rawlsian agents with those actors operating under Smith's notion of sympathy. Smith's conception of the self is 'thicker' than Rawls, meaning there are more characteristics related to their identities and self-knowledge. Many of Rawls' critics argue that his persons are too minimal.[46] It is unlikely, they suggest, that individuals could ever make any decisions without knowing their history, or their moral framework. Smith's theory is not susceptible to this challenge. For Smith, moral adjudication exists in a context. Decisions cannot be made without knowing the relevant histories, and without being aware of the personhood of others. Because of the relational and reflexive nature of Smith's notion of identity, and because an individual's self-image is itself informed by social input, denying the humanity of others results in the denial of one's own humanity. Human beings are too intimately intertwined to function under a veil of ignorance.

The closest Rawls ever comes to the complex reciprocal nature of sympathy is his discussion of *reflective equilibrium*. For Rawls, reflective equilibrium is the balancing of our principles with an intuitive sense that, although our principles say otherwise, an existing situation is clearly unjust or immoral. This may result, according to Rawls, in a shift of understanding as to what our principles of justice should be.[47] This is analogous in many ways to Smith's sympathy. However, Rawls casts doubts on the possibility of reflective equilibrium, and throughout *A Theory of Justice*, the term has more force as a rhetorical tool than as a normative one. For Rawls, reflective equilibrium holds no normative power. For Smith, however, sympathy is that which enables our moral positions to have normativity.

Rawls' moral agents are thin and, perhaps, essentialist. Critics of Rawls, and Rawls himself, have attributed to Smith a similar conception of the self. They see in Smith's impartial spectator a version of the ideal-observer theory, in which an agent who is free from bias can make moral decisions from an Archimedean point of view. This is a misreading of Smith, and recalls our discussion about impartiality in regards to *LRBL*. The impartial spectator is subject to the limitations of the agent who created it. It is informed by community standards and practices. Its creation is a product of a life-long history of sympathy and illustrates that a person's self-image is irrevocably intertwined with the judgments others have made in regards to the agent. It is a creation of the imagination, and is only as reliable as the person whose imagination it is.[48] Smith reminds his readers, "every faculty in one man is the measure by which he judges the like faculty in another. I judge of your sight by my sight, of your ear by my ear, of your reason by my reason " (I.i.3.10) Once again, Smith is emphasizing the separation of individuals and the inability of people to share direct and privileged experiences. To expect that, given human limitations, an individual is capable of having access to universal and perfect judgments is unreasonable. It would be to take the burden of judgment away from the spectator, and to create something that may be more akin to the perfect result of Rousseau's General Will or the perfect reason of Kant's categorical imperative, both of which rely on the capacity for political truths that are objective and authoritative independent of moral actors.

Ideal observer theories, and theories that rely on the primacy of pure reason, reject context by design. Yet, Smith's moral theory is founded on care. It is true that agents are motivated by pleasure in their search for sympathy, but it is the pleasure that is found in relationships that motivates us. The example of the indifferent slave owner shows that affection for others is a precondition for sympathy. This affection is encouraged by our self-love, it is encouraged by education and social pressure, and it is encouraged, as we shall see in chapter four, by government intervention. But it also has, by necessity, elements of concern for others as persons who are deserving of our attention, and who are deserving of effort.

Smith's purpose in *TMS* is to answer two questions. First, he asks what virtue is; and second, he asks how it is acquired. (VII.i.1) Consequently, *TMS* contains both a meta-ethical theory and a moral psychology. Moral psychology has been our main concern in this chapter so far. One adjudicates by tempering one's sentiments to levels prescribed by the community, however, one must also develop a conscience to determine whether the community is correct. Sympathy is the mechanism by which individuals determine the communal judgment and by which an actor tempers his or her sentiments. The impartial spectator is that person one assumes in order to evaluate, and, if need be, counter, societal judgments. Both mechanisms are imperfect because we are fallible and so must be any honest ethical theory. This recognition of infallibility has itself been acknowledged in *Astronomy* where Smith's skepticism was used as a motivating principle for his account of the inevitable succession of incompatible scientific theories.

Smith's second question, asking what virtue is, is dealt with implicitly throughout *TMS*, but only explicitly beginning in Book V. Uncharacteristically for philosophy books, Smith's survey of the major moral theories does not occur at the beginning of the text; it occurs at the conclusion of *TMS* in Book VII. This is, of course, perfectly consistent with Smith's didactic method. His first concern is to establish a general principle and method – that of the possibility of benevolence and the mechanism of sympathy – and only after the generalities are established is he attentive to the particulars.

In Book VI, Smith's discussion begins with a brief account of childhood, and the process by which someone might move from learning the simple lessons of staying away from harm, to becoming the prudent "legislator", that person who represents "the utmost perfection of all intellectual and of all the moral virtues. It is the best head joined to the best heart. It is the most perfect wisdom combined with the perfect virtue" (VI.i.14) For Smith, the great legislator is, of course, for the most part, a fiction since Smith is explicit about the impossibility of infallibility. Smith's skepticism leads him to caution the reader against those who think they are not only the great legislator but those who have devised a moral and political plan refined enough to make moral decisions for others. He writes:

> The man of system, on the contrary, is apt to be very wise in his own conceit; and is often so enumerated with the supposed beauty of his own ideal plan of government, that he cannot suffer the smallest deviation from any part of it... He seems to imagine that he can arrange the different members of a great society with as much ease as the hand arranges the different pieces upon the chess-board. He does not consider that the pieces upon the chess-board have no other principle of motion besides that which the hand impresses upon them; but that in the great 'chess-board' of human society, every single piece has a principle motion of its own, altogether different from that which the legislature might chuse to impress upon it. If those two principles coincide and act in the same direction, the game of human society will go on easy and harmoniously, and is very likely to be happy and successful. If they are opposite or different, the game will go on miserably, and the society must be at all times in the highest degree of disorder. (VI.ii.2.17)

In this comment, Smith is calling attention to the necessity of self-legislation. Notice that 'each piece has a principle motion of its own", and that if each motion is realized human society "will go on easy and harmoniously". It is here that Smith anticipates his political economy and *WN*. Smith could be talking of little other than individual liberty. Yet, this notion of liberty has its history in a more ancient source, that of the Stoic notion of self-command. He writes:

> Every man, as the Stoics used to say, is first and principally recommended to his own care; and every man is certainly, in every respect, fitter and abler to take care of himself than of any

other person. Every man feels his own pleasures and his own pains more sensibly than those of other people. The former are the original sensations; the latter the reflected or sympathetic images of those sensations. The former may be said to be the substance; the latter the shadow. (VI.ii.1.1)

Because each person knows his or her own needs best, that person should be the agent 'principally' responsible for his or her own decisions. Notice that the term "principally" does not rule out the influence of the community, it only claims that the individual should be the final arbiter of that which is best for him- or herself. But Smith's Stoic influence will not accept that knowledge of what is best as enough for a virtuous life. He writes, "rules will not alone enable him to act in this manner: his own passions are very apt to mislead him." (VI.iii.1) Even the wisest of persons, if not "supported by the most perfect self-command" will fail to fulfill his or her duty. (Vi.iii.1)

Smith writes that self-command is not simply a virtue, but that it supplies all other virtues with "their principle luster" (VI.iii.11) In essence, there are, for Smith, three cardinal virtues: *prudence*, *benevolence*, and *justice*. Each is made possible by wisdom and by self-command. Prudence is the care we have for ourselves, as described above in relation to the Stoics. Benevolence is the care we have for others. It is his claim for the existence of benevolence that finds Smith in agreement with Shaftesbury, Hutcheson, and Hume, and in disagreement with Hobbes and Mandeville. Justice is respecting the rights of others, or, in some sense, justice is care for the community both *qua* community and *qua* individuals with boundaries that require respecting. More must be said on justice, but this will be deferred until chapter five, although it will be briefly touched upon below and in chapter four's discussion of *WN*.

There is, of course, a tension between the virtues of prudence and benevolence. Caring for others may bleed into paternalism, and caring for oneself may often entail neglecting others. This is also an economic concern, and in addressing this tension, Smith finds himself influenced by Mandeville's solution to the selfishness that Smith rejects.

Recall the claim that a person is primarily recommended to his or her own care in which Smith charges individuals with their own well-being. Recall also Smith's claim that each chess piece has its own principle of motion, and that each piece, when observed by the chess player, has imposed on it the motion of the hand of the chess player. It is with these two points in mind that the reader should regard Smith's first published reference to the invisible hand.

53

The rich only select from the heap of what is most precious and agreeable. They consume little more than the poor, and in spite of their natural selfishness and rapacity, though they mean only their own conveniency, though the sole end which they propose from the labours of all thousands whom they employ, be the gratification of their own vain and insatiable desires. They are led by an invisible hand to make nearly the same distribution of the necessaries of life, which would have been made, had the earth been divided into equal portions among all its inhabitants, and thus without intending it, without knowing it, advance the interest of the society, and afford means to the multiplication of the species. (IV.i.11)

Smith's claim in this passage is that natural selfishness contributes the to well-being of all, and that given the limited consumption capabilities of the rich, the poor are supplied with their needs, even with the 'rapacity' of the wealthy. Smith, like Mandeville, argues that consumption helps distribute the necessities of life.

This claim necessitates an economic discussion that is best postponed until the next chapter. As stated, it is a hard claim to defend without engaging in a discussions of the free market and the mechanisms designed to maintain justice within that market. Any such defense must incorporate *WN* and I will address this issue in detail throughout chapter four. I caution the skeptical reader to hold off on *economic* judgment for the moment, and consider the philosophical point inherent in this claim, one that becomes visible when this passage is read as an attempt to reconcile the competing needs of benevolence, prudence, and, ultimately, justice. With the doctrine of the invisible hand, Smith is arguing that persons in society are complimentary. It is not the case that one should see society solely in terms of conflict and sacrifice. According to Smith, even at their most selfish, individuals contribute something to the well being of others.

The complementary nature of human interaction is seen throughout Smith's work. There can be no spectator without an actor, there can be no self-understanding without the other, and there can be no individual judgment without the judgment of the community. The mechanism of sympathy has shown repeatedly that moral adjudication and formation of identity is a social process. There will be conflict. However, this conflict does not damn individuals to a brutal war of all against all; it does not necessitate scarcity, nor does it lead to a hostility against the moral judgments of others concluding absurdly with the claim that hell is, in some sense, other people. For Smith, as for Aristotle, *anthropos* is the political animal, and that such is the reality is to be savored and not condemned.

For Smith, prudence, benevolence and justice work together, bolstered by self-command. How are we to know when we are being prudent? How much benevolence is too much? The cardinal virtues are each examples of virtue, but what exactly does Smith mean by virtue? For the answers to these questions, we return to moral psychology. Virtue is that which an impartial spectator approves of, and vice is that which the impartial spectator condemns. Virtue is propriety, informed by the community and balanced by the individual conscience.

Smith argues there are two points when one examines acts: before and after. Individuals tend to be biased in both cases but unfortunately are the most biased when they need to be the least so, for example, when one is forced to make an important but highly charged decision. (III.4.2) Consequently, the propriety of actions is determined after the fact, when one is best able to distance oneself from the emotions and situations that caused them. Retrospective evaluation allows actors to be aware of consequences they were unaware of before the act took place. Utility does play a role in moral adjudication, but it is minimal.

An actor is the most impartial after an act. The actor compares his or her actions to the actions of others and compares his or her respective outcomes to his or her own reactions and to those of the community and makes a judgment as to whether the act was appropriate at the time. This repeated observation of oneself and others allow an individual to form general rules of conduct.

> It is thus that the general rules of morality are formed. They are ultimately founded upon experience of what, in particular instances, our moral faculties, our natural sense of merit and propriety approve... We do not originally approve or condemn particular actions because upon examinations, they appear to be agreeable or inconsistent with a certain general rule. The general rule, on the contrary, is formed, by finding from experience, that all actions of a certain kind, or circumstance in a certain manner are approved or disapproved of. (III.4.8)

For Smith, general rules of conduct arise from examination of our actions and the reflection upon appropriate and inappropriate conduct, not the other way around. Only after the general rules are formed are they used to judge. The general rules are constructs developed from earlier activity and are themselves context-dependent. This is a blatant rejection of the notion that there exists absolute, Archimedean, *a priori* standards in which to judge actions, and would, if taken further, reject the notion that general rules of conduct are handed down, through revelation, by God, or that they must necessarily apply equally, in the same manner, in every case, to every agent. Morality is a product of human reasoning. It is reliable without divine influence, and its standards may differ from situation to situation.

Thus, we see why Smith is in alignment with Shaftesbury and Hutcheson. Like other Enlightenment figures, Smith seeks to divorce morality from religion, and relies upon the natural human capacities for a reliable ethics. Smith also follows Shaftesbury and Hutcheson in associating moral adjudication with feelings. Smith, however does not present us with a moral sense theory. There is not one original intuition that informs a moral agent of that which is appropriate and that which is not. The moral sense theorists offered a singular source for moral adjudication; Smith offers more. He provides a theory of moral sentiments, not a theory of the moral sentiment. There is a multiplicity of sentiments to influence our decisions. Using passions, reasoning, and scientific methodology, in accordance with a well cultivated impartial spectator, the moral agent finds those actions that are praiseworthy, even if the community rejects the acts and withholds praise.

Much more is contained within *TMS* including a critique of utility as the governing ethical consideration, a critique of using wealth as a standard for praise, and a large discussion of that which might corrupt the sentiments. Although some of these topics will be addressed in chapters four and five, much must be left out due to space limitations. The nature of a book such as *On Adam Smith* is to whet the reader's appetite, not to satiate his or her hunger. It is therefore worth noting that Smith's rhetorical skills are such that no secondary source could do justice to the depth and sophistication of *TMS*. It is a wonderful and undervalued philosophical text; it is worth reading on its own.

Nevertheless, *TMS* is incomplete. As made evident by repeated references to unfinished discussions, *TMS* needs more to buttress its claims. A further text is required to complement it, to elaborate on its conclusions, to fill its holes and to clear up its ambiguities. Smith's work – both in 1759, when the first edition was released, and in 1790 when the sixth, radically enlarged, definitive edition was released – requires more than what is found within its covers. Much to the surprise of the philosophical community, that sequel would not be a work of moral philosophy per se. Instead, Smith would write a massive economic treatise that would challenge much of the political wisdom of the day, and in the process, he would change the world.

5

The Wealth of Nations

An Inquiry into the Nature and Causes of the Wealth of Nations was published in 1776; it took Smith twelve years to write. The book was an immediate success. The first edition sold out in six months, and three other editions would follow in Smith's lifetime. Within a few years, taxes suggested in the book were passed in Parliament, and Smith himself became a major consultant in political affairs. The book remains as possibly the most important book in the history of economics, and many give it credit for being the first systematic account of the mechanism of the free market. Its pithy slogans remain in everyday use. Few educated persons are in complete ignorance of Smith's *Laissez Faire* economics, his references to the invisible hand, or his comments regarding the self-interest of the butcher, the brewer and the baker. With the release of *WN*, Smith would become the patron saint of modern 'capitalism', although Smith himself never used the term. Matters are complicated by the fact that, although *WN* is often referred to, it is rarely read. That which is normally ascribed to Smith is frequently inaccurate and rarely complete. The commonplace caricature of Adam Smith's theories has only the most superficial similarities to Smith's actual work.

WN is a massive treatise. The Glasgow edition, released in honor of the 200 anniversary of *WN's* publication, is bound in two volumes and the body of the text is 950 pages long. The index alone spans an additional 61 pages. The language is more technical than *TMS*, and is written in a much dryer style. It contains long statistical passages, and detailed accounts of historical minutiae. Smith no longer communicates as a teacher would; his twelve-year absence from lecturing is quite evident. Although *WN* lacks the rhetorical flourishes and the protreptic pronoun of *TMS*, the voice is clearly Smith's. The arguments are clear and simply written, and Smith still invokes graphic examples and vivid anecdotes.

Of the release of *WN*, in a letter dated April 1, 1776, David Hume wrote:

> *Euge! Belle!* Dear Mr. Smith: I am much please'd with your Performance, and the Perusual of it has taken me from a State of great anxiety. It was a Work of so much Expectation, by yourself, and by the Public, that I trembled for its Appearance; but am now much relieved...it has Depth and Solidarity and Acuteness, and is so much illustrated by curious Facts, that it must at least take the public attention. (*Corr.* 150)

David Hume was clearly pleased with Smith's book, as was the public. In this congratulatory letter to Smith, Hume did take issue with the role of rent in the establishment of natural price, and suggested that Smith underestimated the role of supply and demand, but Hume's comments lack specific detail and Smith's responses aren't forthcoming. Both philosophers were preoccupied with Hume's failing health, and only a few months after *WN*'s publication, Hume passed away.

Central to *WN* is the claim that political and economic liberty are necessary conditions for each other. The cultivation and establishment of one is required for the cultivation and establishment of the other. *WN* is therefore not strictly an economics text. It is, instead, about *political economy*. Smith defines this hybrid science as providing both "a plentiful revenue or subsistence for the people, or more properly to enable them to provide such a revenue or subsistence for themselves" and, the means by which the economy is to "supply the state or commonwealth with a revenue sufficient for the publick services." (IV.intro.1)

In *WN*, Smith sought to analyze the healthy economy and the political principles upon which it would be based. This included a blueprint of the structure and economic activities that support the state while ensuring that its political and economic arrangement did not inhibit justice, liberty or interfere with individual or collective morality. It is these latter concerns that have been the most overlooked, until fairly recently, in Smith studies. Classical economic theory tends to read *WN* as separate from Smith's non-economic work, yet Smith himself understood the two books as systematic. He was deeply concerned with the ways in which the economy could contribute to the intellectual and moral flourishing of those who are subject to it. As evidence to Smith's loyalty to his moral system, he continued to revise *TMS* long after *WN's* publication, and, of the two, he is reported to have regarded TMS as "much superior".

The dominant school of economic thought prior to the publication of *WN* was mercantilism. Mercantilists argued that a nation's wealth was to be measured by the amount of money contained within its borders at any one time. They were anti-trade and anti-competition. Smith would challenge that view. In *WN,* he argued that a nation's wealth was to be measured in the quantification of the collective labor of its workers, including the cumulative effect of trade, and the capacity for continual economic advancement. According to mercantilism, a country with few resources but a large workforce would not be considered wealthy. Smith's theory suggested that work hours should be incorporated into the measure of a country's value.

For Smith, economic growth is best cultivated under a 'division of labor', the process by which workers complete discrete tasks that, when connected, result in the completed manufacture of a product. This is to be compared with a more holistic labor practice in which workers create an entire product on their own. Smith argues that the former is exponentially more efficient than the latter. Citing the eighteen processes involved in making pins, Smith writes:

> A workman not educated to this business (which the division of labour has rendered a distinct trade), nor acquainted with the use of the machinery employed in it (to the invention of which the same division of labour has probably given occasion), could scarce, perhaps, with the utmost industry make one pin in a day, and certainly could not make twenty. But in the way in which this business is now carried on ... ten persons ... could make among them upwards of forty-eight thousand pins in a day. Each person, therefore, making a tenth part of forty-eight thousand pins, might be considered as making four thousand eight hundred pins in a day. (I.i.3)

According to Smith, under the division of labor, workers, when assigned individual but complementary tasks, succeed in raising production output. This, in turn, improves income, economic stability, and wages. Smith elaborates on this efficiency, providing an account of the wasted energy involved in moving from one skill to another, yet at the core of this discussion is an argument regarding the methodological advantages of specialization in all of its forms. Smith argues that division of labor, in addition to increasing productivity "in every art" (I.1.4), also increases intellectual advancement and understanding. He writes:

> Men are more likely to discover easier and readier methods of attaining any object, when the whole attention of their minds is directed towards that single object, than when it is dissipated among a great variety of things. But in the consequences of the division of labour, the whole of every man's attention comes naturally directed towards some one very simple object. It is naturally to be expected, therefore that some one or other of those who are employed in each particular branch of labour should soon find out easier and readier methods of performing their own particular work, wherever the nature of it admits of such improvement. (I.i.8)

In arguing for the intellectual efficiency of the division of labor, Smith is arguing for the advancement of specialization. According to Smith, it is those who are most familiar with processes that innovate. In providing evidence for this claim, he cites a particularly vivid example of a young boy who, while engaged by a fire department for a menial task, sought to create more playtime, and discovered a laborsaving device in the first fire engines. (I.1.8)

Smith emphasizes that the division of labor is not simply a technological concern. Intellectual activities are also to be specialized. Accordingly, even "philosophy or speculation becomes, like every other employment, the principle or sole trade and occupation of a particular class of citizens". (I.1.9)

For Smith, a strong economy is not just stabile; it is progressive. An increase in the revenue and stock (capital) of each nation increases the national wealth, which, in turn, increases wages. (I.vii.22) By highlighting the division of labor, Smith hopes that improved efficiency and increased innovation will advance the economy, and his goal was to create an economy in which such increases are perpetual. However, the term 'division of labor' is rhetorically misleading. The grammatical structure of the sentence makes labor the subject, and emphasizes the modifier. There is, however, an unarticulated word in the phrase. H*uman* labor is of concern here. If we change perspective, we can also understand the "division of [human] labor" as the "conjoining of [human] labor". In is "conjoined" because division of labor only functions when specialized individuals work together in an intentionally coordinated fashion. Thus, we are once again confronted with Smith's notion from *TMS* that human life is complementary. Any advancement that results from the division of labor is the direct product of people working together, with special attention to the ways in which each person is to interact with each other person.

In the pooling of human resources, one sees a qualitative as well as a quantitative shift. In addition to adding efficiency, the conjoining of labor creates, in a certain sense, a community with a shared goal. The labor required by each individual worker is no longer identifiable in the final product in any discrete way. Take, for example, the Amish practice of barn raising, in which the efficiency of the conjoined labor results in the erection of a barn in the fraction of the time that individuals alone could accomplish the same act. Barn raising is a distinctly social act. The unifying nature of the ritual becomes intuitively clear when one imagines the absurd instance of a worker identifying which of the countless nails used in the barn he himself had hammered.[49] Such an attempt at identifying one's own labor would be a violation of the spirit and meaning of the enterprise. It would disregard that the barn is in some very important sense, more than the sum of its parts.

A critic may argue that contemporary practices in the division of labor create isolated atomistic individuals, and that community is destroyed and not created by Smith's model of production. Smith would be sympathetic to such an argument. He is explicit in his comments that the division of labor tends towards the destruction of creativity and identity. As discussed throughout this book, Smith will take great pains to address the negative effects of a free-market economy and to rectify any injustices inherent in the system. The negative effects of division of labor are countered, in particular, by mandatory education. This will be addressed shortly.

Because the division of labor has labor as its subject, it is easy to evaluate the outcome in terms of efficiency, and certainly that is Smith's main point. However, the phrase, "the conjoining of [human] labor" allows analysts to see Smith's commitment to social and intellectual advancement as well as efficiency. Efficiency is a form of improvement. As we have already seen in *Astronomy*'s account of the progress of knowledge, as well as in *TMS*'s account of the advancement of virtue, Smith has a deep commitment to the improvement of the condition of both the individual and the community as a whole.

Smith is explicit regarding the connection between the division of labor, the community it creates, and the improvement of the human condition. He writes:

> As it is this disposition which forms the difference of talents, so remarkable among men of different professions, so it is this same disposition which renders that difference useful. Many tribes of animals acknowledged to be all of the same species, derive from nature a much more remarkable distinction of genius, than what, antecedent to custom, and education, appears to take place among men. By nature a philosopher is not in genius and disposition half so different from a street porter, as a mastiff is from a greyhound, or a greyhound from a spaniel, or this last from a shepherd's dog. Those different tribes of animals, however, though all of the same species, are of scarce use to one another... The effects of those different geniuses and talents, for want of the power or disposition to barter and exchange, cannot be brought into common stock, and do not in the least contribute to the better accommodation and conveniency of the species. Each animal is still obliged to support and defend itself separately and independently... Among men, on the contrary, the most dissimilar geniuses are of use to one another...being brought, as it were, into common stock, where every man may purchase whatever part of the produce of other men's talents he has occasion for. (I.ii.5)

Smith's focus on improvement is most evident in WN. He argues that the wealth of a nation can be identified, at least in part, by examining the standard of living of the poorest members of society. He further states that a society with a better situated poor class is to be preferred over a society with a worse situated poor class. In that regard, Smith anticipated Rawls' *maximin* principle by almost 200 years.

Smith was very much concerned with *universal opulence*, a situation in which all members of society are regarded as having adequate, if not substantial, wealth. He writes:

> Servants and labourers and workmen of different kinds, make up the far greater part of every great political society. But what improves the circumstances of the greater part can never be

regarded as an incoveniency to the whole. No society can surely be flourishing and happy, of which the far greater part of the members are poor and miserable. It is but equity, besides, that they who feed, cloath and lodge the whole body of the people, should have such a share of the produce of their own labour as to be themselves tolerably well fed, cloathed and lodged (I.viii.36)

Again, compare Smith's defense of the maximization of the wealth in the lowest economic rung with Rawls' original position in *A Theory of Justice*. Rawls justifies the *maximin* principle by appealing to the risk that those agents in the original position take when they create society. Those deliberating choose the best society out of fear for their own lot in life. In the above selection, however, Smith's motivations are not selfish. He appeals to the happiness of the society as a whole. People cannot be happy when others are miserable. Perhaps more importantly, Smith also appeals to justice. Equity, not self-interest, demands that workers have a tolerable life. Furthermore, Smith is explicit that wages below the level needed for "maintenance" are not "consistent with common humanity". (I.viii.16). Once again, it is not self-interest that drives certain economic concerns, it is an appeal to a normative ethical standard of decency.

For Smith, universal opulence is a product of the division of labor. It is the cumulative effect of the labor of the vast numbers of members of society. It results in the advancement of any one individual's quality of life. He writes:

Observe the accommodation of the most common artificer or day labourer in a civilized thriving country and you will perceive the number of people of whose industry a part, though but a small part, has been employed in procuring for him this accommodation, exceeds all computation. The woolen coat, for example, which covers the day labourer, as course and rough as it may appear, is the produce of the joint labour of a great multitude of workmen. The shephard, the sorter of the wool, the wool-comber or carder, the dyer, the scribbler, the spinner, the weaver, the fuller, the dresser,... how many merchants and carriers besides...to say nothing of such complicated machines of the ship of the sailor, the mill of the fuller, or even the loom of the weaver... the miner, the builder of the furnace... the feller of the timber.... Without the assistance and cooperation of many thousands, the very meanest person in a civilized country could not be provided, even according to, what are falsely imagined, the easy and simple manner in which he is commonly accommodated. Compared, indeed with the more extravagant luxury of the great, his accommodation must no doubt appear extremely simple and easy; and yet it may be true, perhaps that the accommodation of a European prince does not always so much exceed that of an industrious and frugal peasant, as the accommodation of the later exceed that of many an African king, the absolute master of the lives and liberties of ten thousand naked savages. (I.i.10-11)

Ignoring the ethnocentric language that was a product of the time, Smith's point is that division of labor makes the material quality of life better for all, and that the inequities of a commercial society are not nearly as dramatic as the inequities in a non-commercial society. Smith goes through great pains to discuss the historical progression of society through its stages. He shows how these advancements contributed to greater freedoms and greater rights. For example, trade, Smith argues, is directly responsible for the shift from feudal systems to systems in which tenants have rights and control over their own land. (III.iv.10) Free trade is therefore to be encouraged, even if it means importing cheaper goods. (IV.ii.12) Free trade promotes liberty and national wealth. Contrary to the mercantilist argument that it is in the national interest to both keep wealth within national borders and to inhibit the economic growth of other nations, Smith explicitly argues that wealthy nations are to be valued since they can contribute to trade and thereby increase the wealth of all in their vicinity. (IV.iii.c.11) Since liberty is the product of the advancement of trade, wealthy neighbors are also politically advantageous. Although Smith does caution that wealthy neighbors are harder to defeat in times of war, the direct connection between trade and liberty makes the promotion of wealth outside of national borders a matter of the cultivation of freedom.

The advancement of individual liberty was surely not the intent of the landowners who opened their hearts to trade, nor was it the intention of those who sought international trade relations. It was an unintended consequence, just as universal opulence is an unintended consequence of the free market. Smith's second most famous observation reminds us that individuals, when engaged in market activities, are concerned primarily with their own advancement and not with secondary concerns such as universal opulence. He writes: "It is not from the benevolence of the butcher, the brewer and the baker, that we expect our dinner, but from their regard to their own interest. We address ourselves, not to their humanity but to their self-love, and never talk to them of our own necessities but of their advantages." (WN I.ii.2)

However, as can be seen throughout this book, it is *only* in market activity that self-interest governs. Smith's observation is not a general claim about all human action; it is only a claim about economic motivation. Because sympathy is a natural tendency, individuals are compelled to care about others regardless of their tendencies towards the market. This insures that moral consideration is always prior to self-interest. For Smith, identity is itself a product of sympathy. Self-interest itself could not exist without sympathetic understanding of others. Therefore, self-interest is a choice, not an inevitability. Given the predilection of people to falsely associate Smith with a purely selfish human nature, it is worth reminding the reader that from the very first line of *TMS*, Smith has consistently defended the existence of benevolence.

It is the beneficial yet unintended consequences that Smith seeks to highlight with his most famous metaphor, the invisible hand. Smith uses it to emphasize that most often, more good is done by promoting one's own self-interest than by trying to manipulate society for the betterment of the whole. According to Smith, the invisible hand will direct the common good when we each concern ourselves with our immediate duties and responsibilities. In *The Theory of Moral Sentiments*, we saw that Smith had faith in the natural division of necessities. In the excerpt highlighted in chapter three, Smith tells us that the rich, in working to provide for their own selfish need, supply jobs and income for the poor. According to Smith, an unintended consequence of this is that goods are divided among members of society in roughly the same manner that they would have been if nature itself had divided it with an eye towards fairness.

As stated earlier, this is a difficult claim to defend. At first glance, it seems patently false that the division of goods is not consolidated unfairly in the wealthy. The modern world is full of examples in which the wealthy have so much more than the poor do, that such a notion seems laughable if not offensive. Yet, in defense of Smith, it should be emphasized that Smith argues that it is "necessaries" – or in contemporary terms, necessities – that are distributed fairly, and it is not luxuries that he claims are justly distributed. Smith is little concerned with luxuries. In *TMS*, he argues that the rich are ridiculously over attentive to luxury and that it is a sign of bad character to be so. In *WN*, he critically claims, "with the greater part of rich people, the chief enjoyment of riches consists in the parade of riches, which in their eyes is never so compleat as when they appear to posses those decisive marks of opulence which nobody can posses but themselves". (I.xi.c.31) In this regard, Smith always writes with a critical tone.

Smith also acknowledges the social division that comes from economic inequality, as well as the governmental power it necessitates. He writes:

> wherever there is great property, there is great inequality. For one very rich man, there must be at least five hundred poor.... It is only under the shelter of the civil magistrate that the owner of the valuable property....can sleep a single night in security. He is at all times surrounded by unknown enemies...from whose injustice he can be protected only by the powerful arm of the civil magistrate." (V.i.b.2)

The rich have a need for government that the poor do not share. Civil government "supposes a certain subordination", and "the principle causes which naturally introduce subordination gradually grow up with the growth of that valuable property". (V.i.b.3)

There are two ways to consider the preceding comments. The first is that the poor have no scruples; they would steal that which is not theirs. The second is that excessive wealth is unjust; hostility is caused by inequity. Both shed light on Smith's point. Smith does draw a connection between poverty and crime. However, he argues that this connection is a direct result of the corruption of the sentiments. According to Smith, it is inequity and poverty that cause corruption. He writes:

> The disposition to admire, and almost worship, the rich and the powerful, and to despise, or at least, to neglect persons of poor and mean condition, though necessary both to establish and to maintain the distinction of ranks and the order of society, is, at the same time, the great and most universal cause of the corruption of our moral sentiments. That wealth and greatness are often regarded with the respect and admiration which are due only to wisdom and virtue; and that the contempt, of which vice and folly are the only proper objects, is often most unjustly besytowed upon poverty and weakness, has been the complaint of moralists of all ages. (*TMS* I.iii.3.2)

In this paragraph, Smith is as explicit as he gets. Poverty and its consequent subordination are the major cause of the corruption of the sentiments. This in turn interferes with sympathy. By definition, anything that interferes with sympathy is immoral. In his discussion of poverty and crime, Smith shifts back and forth from making empirical claims to making systematic ones. He uses the observations about the poor to attach the facts of society to the motivations for particular forms of social organization. As discussed in reference to *Astronomy*, for Smith, systems are always the product of the imagination, and the identification of a systematic order is always regarded as part of the understanding. Consequently, as Smith's comments about the poor are empirical and systematic, they are also educative.

Such comments are made by Smith as a way of triggering sympathy. By identifying the character faults that lie within the greedy and the vain, and by pointing out the cause of sentimental corruption in the poor, Smith hopes to educate his readers. Recall from the discussion of Shaftesbury in *LRBL,* that any study of ethics has a pedagogical role. By recounting a theory, the author is, in some sense, teaching. Had Smith relied upon a falsely ornate rhetoric that inhibited sympathy, he would have been as worthy of condemnation as Shaftesbury was. However, since Smith is plain and graphic in his enumeration of the harm caused by greed, vanity, and oppression, he can be regarded, by his own standards, as communicating a virtuous character.

Most important, a defense of Smith's claim must rest on the understanding that Smith's faith in market-driven distributive justice is only plausible given a market supported by certain specific social and governmental structures that provide for, in contemporary terms, an equal playing field. The design towards universal opulence is one such structure, and others will be discussed shortly, but at least one element of such a system is political and philosophical education, often in the forms of didactic treatises. Since *WN* is designed to educate, it can be seen, by Smith, as part of the solution.

Nevertheless, even the Smithean must acquiesce to criticism in this regard. The self-correcting nature of the market is far from foolproof. If the only criticism of public assistance programs is faith in the natural distribution of the market, then even the most steadfast supporters of Smith must encourage their creation. The growth of worldwide capitalism has left many without access to most if not all necessities. Amidst the wealthiest metropolis lie regions of desperate poor whose future prospects are frustrated by political apathy, marginalization and ignorance from all sectors of the *polis*. They have neither the sympathies of the communities they are oppressed by, nor the political powers to influence change from within. It is this social separation that Smith cautions us against in *TMS* as he reminds us that humans are communal creatures, and that one must cultivate all people if one is to cultivate any one person. However, a Smithean must also insist that much of the cause of such inequalities is the steadfast adherence to the greedy and selfish caricature of Smith's free market that passes for economic education, as well as the utter neglect of many of the market's supporting mechanisms.

In light of the unfortunate injustices of the contemporary world, Smith would caution his readers to temper their tendencies towards social engineering. Whatever public assistance programs one designs for the betterment of society as a whole, Smith believes that one should not force benevolence on those activities that are not suited for it. Reminiscent of Mandeville's comments in *Fable of the Bees*, Smith emphasizes that the very point of the free-market system is that it does not require altruistic motivations when constructed properly. He writes that the individual, generally:

> neither intends to promote the publick interest, nor knows how he is promoting it... He intends only his own security; and by directing that industry in such a manner as its produce may be of the greatest value, he intends only his own gain, and he is in this, as in many other cases, led by an invisible hand to promote an end which was no part of his intention. Nor is it always the worse for the society that it was no part of it. By pursuing his own interest he frequently promotes that of society more effectively than when he really intends to promote it. (IV.ii.9)

Throughout *LRBL*, *Astronomy*, and *TMS*, Smith has attempted to project a sense of Newtonian design on observable facts. Smith continued this method by beginning *WN* with a declaration of the general principle that economic growth is the product of the division of labor. The human desire to provide systematic explanation is, for Smith, inevitable. Yet, with this third reference to the invisible hand, Smith tempers the passion for system. He criticizes the "man of system" who sees order where there is none, and who, because of the aesthetic appeal towards design, attempts to forces society to mold to a fiction.

Recall Smith's discussion of the chessboard from *TMS*. In this caution against manipulation, we see the origin of what is perhaps the greatest misunderstanding of Smith's theories. Many have interpreted his distrust in systems, his faith in the invisible hand, and his discussion of limited government as evidence that Smith's theories are quasi-libertarian, or that Smith, in contemporary terms, is more socially conservative than he really is. Although government does play a limited role in Smith's system, it does not abandon the populace solely to its own devices. It is only in the most economically oriented arenas that the role of government is limited, and Smith justifies limitations only to the point where the state remains capable of creating a solid foundation to counter the inherently divisive aspects of the free market. The market is only acceptable to Smith when society is structured to promote justice, rights and morality.

Libertarians argue, "the government is the most dangerous institution known to man".[50] They claim the only justified role of government "is that of the protector of the citizens against aggression by other individuals,... it should never initiate aggression, [it is the] embodiment of *retaliatory* use of force against anyone who initiates it".[51] Libertarians reject any laws that are paternalistic or that require citizens to assist one another. They reject the notion that any activity that does not harm others should be prohibited, and they reject the notion that citizens should be required to pay for public assistance programs. They argue that taxes are a violation of property rights. Except, perhaps, for the prevention of monopolies – and that too is controversial -- the libertarian state is minimalist. Libertarians believe that the free-market can regulate itself without *any* government intervention. According to this perspective, the sovereign power must remain wholly separate from the economic activity of its citizens.

The role of the state in a libertarian society is representative of a lack of moral obligation between individuals. Since there is no compelling reason why one must do anything other than respect the rules of entitlement, libertarians believe that to require the citizen to engage in anything other than recognition and respect of entitlement rules is an abuse of the power of the state.

Adam Smith also argues for a minimalist state; however, he is not as minimal as the libertarian view. Smith sees the state as having three duties. They are: to protect the society from violence and invasion by other societies; to protect every member of the society from the injustice or oppression of every other member, or, as Smith calls it, to establish "the exact administration of justice"; and, to erect and maintain public works and institutions the cost of which are too great and the benefit of which are too small for an individual or small group to finance. (IV.ix.51) These public goods include armies, police, public works, public schools, and religious education. Although some radical libertarians would challenge state-supported police and public works, for the most part, it is the third function of the state, the maintenance of public goods, that differs from libertarianism. It is the meaning of distributive justice, which is ambiguous enough to pull Smith further from social conservatism than some might otherwise suggest.

Furthermore, in the list of duties of the sovereign, the term 'public goods' is itself a matter of great controversy, and Smith has no particular attachment to a minimalist conception of it. In combination with more modern conceptions of justice, Smith's theories are perfectly compatible with a more inclusive notion of public good.

It is true that Smith has great faith in the self-corrective and self-regulatory aspects of the free-market. However, it is a mistake to consider *WN* or Smith's project as a whole as purely *laissez faire* without any concern for the injustice of economic inequalities. Throughout his work, Smith does provide prescriptions that help reduce the divisions between classes. In doing so, he presupposes his moral theories. Jeremy Z. Muller, in *Adam Smith in his Time and Ours*, states it well when he claims that Smith, "argued against government involvement less as a matter of *principle* than as a matter of *strategy*, and he was willing to depart from that strategy when there were compelling reasons..."[52]

Smith argues that in a commercial society, every person becomes *in some sense* a merchant. (I.iv.1) In this regard, all individuals can influence all others because *in some sense* they must be consumers. Frequent competitive trade leads to honesty because, as he writes elsewhere, "whenever dealings are frequent, a man does not expect to gain so much by any one contract as by probity and punctuality in the whole, and a prudent dealer who is sensible of his real interest, would rather choose to lose what he has a right to than give any ground for suspicion". (LJ(B).328) The economic pressure towards prudence – one of the cardinal virtues in *TMS* – is more powerful for the merchants than for the aristocracy since the aristocrats have much less to lose than the shopkeeper; they can afford mischief since they have so much to spare. According to Smith, the more bound up one is in commercial society, the more one is subject to the standards of good business. Furthermore, Smith argues, the wise merchant knows that a successful business is a tenuous enterprise and that prudence will improve the chances of success.

This promotion of honesty in contracts is one example of Smith's faith that the market encourages virtuous activity. In *TMS*, Smith argues that success in the market depends on "the favour and good opinion of their neighbors and equals" and as we have seen, the requisite good opinion of others is essential in moral activity since it is a consequence of sympathy. (*TMS* I.iii.3.5) In contrast, non-commercial societies depend, "not upon the esteem of the intelligent and well-informed equals, but upon the fanciful and foolish favour of the ignorant" and, "flattery and falsehood too often prevail over merit and abilities." (*TMS* I.iii.3.6) Here we see that for Smith, it is a "well-informed" equal that is most valued, and not simply an equal. Smith's major concern is to create a well-informed populace. He does this through a market system built upon government intervention.

The importance of these virtue-producing mechanisms needs to be emphasized. Without them, Smith's economic theories *are* divisive. There is, for example, no discussion in *WN* Book I, II, or III of any mechanism that helps cultivate justice or that provides opportunities to those without the means, either economic or intellectual, of entering the market-place. Smith discusses these issues separately, yet at least one very popular edition of the *WN* contains only the first three books.[53] Book V of the Wealth of Nations is both a theory of equality of opportunity and a discussion of how services provided by the government can provide equal access without limiting individual freedoms to any large extent.

Smith is insistent throughout his work that those who participate in any activity have more responsibility to contribute to their funding than those who do not. He enumerates the financial burdens of the state as well as those who are responsible for contributions. The defense of society and the chief magistrate should both be publicly funded through taxation: their existence affects everyone; all should contribute. (V.i.i.1) Although this argument may also apply to the administration of justice, the main financial burden should fall upon those who actually use the courts (V.i.i.3) Only in those instances where those convicted do not have the available funds to pay should society as a whole carry the burden. Cost incurred by local towns and provinces should be paid for by the members of the town or province that incur them and not the general community. The maintenance of roads and communications should be contributed to by the community as a whole but more so by those who use them more often. The list continues.

Again, *WN* is not purely *laissez faire*. Throughout the work, Smith provides prescriptions that help reduce the increasing divisions between classes. In both instructions for taxation listed above, maintenance of the court system and maintenance of the road, Smith offers a method that allows the burden of cost to be lifted from those who are unable to contribute.

To elaborate, we can return to the notion of a well-informed populace. In *WN*, Smith argues that it is the state's obligation to protect the "great body of people" and to help them "exert their understanding." (V.i.f.50) Smith is clear that a major difference between individuals is their education. (I.ii.4) He also acknowledges that the division of labor is destructive to intelligence. He writes:

71

But the understandings of the greater part of men are necessarily formed by their ordinary employments. The man whose whole life is spent in performing a few simple operations, of which the effects too are, perhaps, always the same, or very nearly the same, has no occasion to exert his understanding, or to exercise his invention in finding out expedients for removing difficulties which never occur. He naturally loses, therefore, the habit of such exertion, and generally becomes as stupid and ignorant as it is possible for a human creature to become. (V.i.f.50)

It is part of Smith's system to counter the destructive aspects of the free market system, and Smith is explicit that the state is required to counter its negative intellectual effects. To fulfill this responsibility, the government must educate the masses. Smith believes, therefore, that the state should provide incentives to encourage parents to educate their children. Smith recounts the ancient Roman "law of Solon" that released those children whose parents did not assure them the proper education from the responsibility of caring for their parents during their old age. (V.i.f.43) For Smith, education seems to be the line of continuity between generations and to properly educate one's child is a grave and central responsibility of any parent.[54]

For Adam Smith, education helps bridge the gap between the classes. It is a necessity to which both the wealthy and the poor should have access. The wealthy will be compelled to educate themselves and their children because of both "status and reason." Again, we see the product of the social influence of sympathy. Since they can afford it, the wealthy should pay their own way through school. In contrast, the education of the poor will be paid for by the state. Smith writes, "for a very small expense the public can facilitate, can encourage, and can even impose upon almost the whole body of the people, the necessity of acquiring those most essential parts of the education". (V.i.f.54) Society, as a whole, will contribute money, but in order to ensure competition and quality of education, those who attend school will also be required to pay a small fee to their teachers.

For Smith, funding of public educational institutions for the young is a well-regarded trade-off. The cost of educating the poor is small. Smith believed that the logistics behind it are simple and easy. He saw education as a tool for equality, stability, and self-respect. He also believed that specific subjects – reading writing, arithmetic, philosophy, and science – are necessary foundations since they promote skill and reduce ignorance, superstition, and religious fanaticism. He saw these three vices as leading to factionalism that made a society less stable.

Smith wrote extensively on education for both children and adults. Educational institutions can help instill the proper knowledge and self-image in children at a young age, but as children grow, they are more susceptible to different and even more dangerous forces. It is for this reason that Smith believes the sovereign has no small interest in supporting and guiding religious education as well. Religious education, when structured correctly, instills virtue in believers that the market cannot supply. For Smith, the institutions of the market and of secular and religious education are complementary. The market could not exist without the virtue that comes with knowledge and belief.

The problem of religion has its roots in Plato's dialogues, specifically *Republic* and the notion of "the noble lie", and *Laws*. Plato and Smith's concern is that allegiance to religious organization is more intimately felt than loyalty of the states. A powerful religion is therefore a danger to political stability and social cohesiveness. By supporting scientific and philosophical education, Smith hopes to counter suspicion, but by supporting religious education of a certain type, Smith hopes to use religious sentiment to strengthen loyalty to the state by associating justice and morality with "the deity", thereby making believers less likely to challenge the law. Smith also develops an elaborate structure in which to weed out the most fanatical religions. It is a process of competition analogous to the free market. This, in conjunction with secular and religious education will ensure, Smith believes, that citizens are religious enough to be loyal to the state, but not so much so that they chose their own sect over their political commitments. [55]

The key to cultivating sympathy is education. Moral actors must learn to understand and treat others morally by being educated about them. We must learn their stories, we must learn their histories, and we must understand their personhood. Yet, the ability to learn about others is dependant on the ability to learn. This ability is, at least in part, a product of formal education. Smith understands that morality will have no influence over the population, and the state will be one of poor and uninformed character, if the members of the state are unable to see each other as having essential dignity and worth. Sympathy, in conjunction with the imagined impartial spectator, is that mechanism, however limited, that provides the accumulation of moral knowledge in the form of a conscience. This knowledge gives individuals self-awareness enough to challenge those social conclusions that they disagree with. Smith needs the impartial spectator to encapsulate the life long learning and the moral conclusions that will inform an individual's actions.

According to Smith, the lack of education is as much a barrier to being sympathized with as being able to sympathize. Those without education are both looked upon with contempt and are denied happiness. (V.i.f.61) Smith compares two individuals, one who is "mutilated of the mind" and one who is "mutilated of the body". He writes of the one who is mutilated of the mind that, "[he] is evidently the more wretched and miserable of the two, because happiness and misery, which reside altogether in the mind, must necessarily depend more upon the healthful or unhealthful, the mutilated state of the mind, than upon that of the body". (V.i.f.60) The person who is denied education is denied ease of sympathy.

The morality of Smith's economics also depends upon education. The market is only just if people, as consumers, participate under conditions of informed consent. Deception destroys the justice of the market. Informed consent, a term Smith does not use, is encapsulated in the notion of price. The *natural* price of a good or service is that price which is the lowest price for which the commodity can be exchanged for without loss. Or, as Smith writes, the natural price is "what it really costs for a person who brings it to market". (I.viii.5) The *market* price is that price for which a product is actually sold for by the merchant. It fluctuates based upon the available goods and the demand for those goods. Smith, however insists that the market price is always "gravitating" or "tending" towards the natural price. (I.vii.15) For Smith, the term 'natural' is not descriptive, it is normative. The natural price is that price a commodity ought to be. According to Smith, when the natural price and the market price are the same, the market is working properly.

It is interesting that the definition of natural price does not include profit. In fact, Smith's discussion of profit is noticeably separate from his discussion of price. Clearly, profit is part of the motivation for why a merchant chooses to sell a commodity, and Smith has elaborate discussions as to what costs are incorporated in the estimation of natural price. They include relevant wages, the profit involved in the material used in the commodity, and relevant rent charges. Although the natural price incorporates profit in regards to material necessary for production, profit received by the sale of the finished product is not included in these calculations. One is forced to wonder whether profit is somehow 'unnatural', and whether or not this is implicitly one of Smith's many criticisms of greed.

Notice also the similarities between natural price and the Stoic notion of law and nature. For the Stoics, all natural events follow laws, and the philosophers sought to enumerate those laws in order to temper their emotion while more consciously coordinating their activities with the natural law. For Smith, as for the Stoics, one can identify the natural law as a normative standard. Price *should not* be arbitrary, nor should it be the product of desires, or simply of supply and demand. The law of natural price tells the consumer that the price should be the actual cost of manufacture. To pay a different price is to pay the *wrong* price.

We can see that education allows the consumer to have a better understanding of the market price and whether it is in alignment with the normative standard. Natural price, then, is the economic analogue of the impartial spectator. It encapsulates all related knowledge. As always, there is a danger in this comparison that the reader may revert to a conception of the impartial spectator as an ideal observer theory, especially since natural price seems to be implicitly Archimedean. It must be emphasized that this is not the case. The consumer is limited in his or her *awareness* of the natural price in the same way that the impartial spectator is limited in its ability to make moral judgments. All judgments are the product of human reason, and human reason is limited.

A discussion of price necessitates a discussion of the relationship between labor and value, where labor is "the real measure of the exchangeable value of commodities". (I.v.1) Smith argues that, historically, labor was the first means of exchange, and that it remains "the ultimate and real standard by which the value of all commodities can at all times and places be estimated and compared." (I.v.7) Yet, labor is an impractical means for exchange. It is reliable as standard of value in principle, but it is hard to measure practically. Therefore, Smith offers a temporal regression that leads, as a chain, towards money. After beginning the chain with a discussion of the value of labor, Smith argues that "corn" is a better measure of value from "century to century" because, as a crop with a clear need for care and harvest, such produce is easily identifiable in terms of labor. "Silver" is an easier standard from "year to year" because silver is easily stored, transported, and measured given a particular standard. (I.v.17)

Smith's labor theory of value is essential because it rests in the core of his objection to mercantilism. Smith argued that the wealth of a nation is the quantified value of labor, and not the amount of money within national borders. Yet, to make this claim, he needed an objective standard by which to value labor. Hence, the value theory of labor: a theory that is, in principle, derived from natural laws in just the same way that price is derived.

Smith also needed a way to convert labor into exchange. Labor cannot be transferred from person to person, nor can it be accumulated for future use. However, most economic interactions involve exchange and not direct manufacture. Without the capacity to quantify and transfer labor, individuals would be trapped and subject to both their own physical limitations, and the whims of immediate need. Smith writes,

> When the division of labour has been once thoroughly established, it is but a very small part of a man's wants which the produce of his own labour can supply. He supplies the far greater part of them by exchanging the surplus part of the produce of his own labor, which is over and above his own consumption, for such parts of the produce of other men's labour as he has occasion for. Every man thus lives by exchanging, or becoming in some measure a merchant, and the society itself grows to be what is properly a commercial society. (I.iv.1)

The objective value of labor is yet another bridge between economic and political liberty. Recall that according to Smith, historically, government has been established for the purpose of protecting the rich and their property. Smith argues, "the property which every man has in his own labor, as it is the original foundation of all property, so is the most sacred and inviolable". (I.x.c.12) As labor is an economic and political concept, it is cultivated by the fluctuations of the marker and inhibited by its inefficiencies. Labor, as property, must be transferable or there can be no liberty in any meaningful sense.

Proper fluctuations of the market are indicative of a state of perfect liberty. Smith offers a dual definition of such liberty. First, perfect liberty is that situation in which a person "may change his trade as often as he pleases". (I.vii.6) Second, perfect liberty is that situation in which the natural price and the market price are in agreement with one another. (I.vii.30). This also serves as a reminder as to the relationship between political and economic freedom. One is not possible without the other. Additionally, it serves as an indication that monopolies are not only infringements upon the market; they are infringements upon liberty. Monopolies interfere with trade which in turn interferes with price and quality. They also inspire unjust laws and taxes. A paradigmatic example of the unjust monopoly is the East India Tea Company, the export company that acted as the chief agent in Britain's colonial struggles with India. In an effort to forestall the company's bankruptcy, Britain granted East India a monopoly over tea sales in the American colonies, declared the tea taxable, and thus inspired the 1773 Boston Tea Party. The monopoly the company held over trade in India resulted in poor quality, limited supply and ultimately, political turmoil. Smith was correctly skeptical when he expressed his doubt that the company would survive in the long run. (V.i.e.30)

Political liberty is intertwined with economic liberty. Each is dependant on education, which is itself dependant upon the sentiments. Sentiments are cultivated and tempered through sympathy. The market is driven by self-interest, yet it is the most effective when self-interest is limited to the market arena. The tendency towards honesty and the requirement of informed consent that are the products of the market can both be used as a force to cultivate virtue among merchants and consumers. The cultivation of virtue is the cultivation of sympathy. It has also been suggested that the division of labor is poorly named. By understanding that efficient labor is a communal activity, one sees the potential for unity and not division in the process of joint manufacture. True unity, the particularly *human* unity, does not take place without sympathy.

Sympathy is self-correcting. The interactions between the individual and the community allow for moral regulation, self-awareness, and conscience. In this same way, the market is also self-correcting, but only given the conditions of support Smith describes. This should be emphasized. It is the moral foundation of sympathy that allows for a just market place, and the institution of the market is itself an instrument that cultivates morality by curbing our tendency toward self-interest and impropriety. Moral individuals will not allow self-love to eclipse their ability to abide by the judgment of that impartial spectator whose role it is to cultivate good moral decision-making, because consumers are always to be understood as persons first and consumers second. In those times that merchants disregard this fact, the merchants are harmed far worse than the individual consumer. Such is the unintended consequence of vicious action as illustrated by the doctrine of the invisible hand. It is a forceful reminder of the worth of others.

Humans are not simply *homo economics* for Smith; they are only sometimes so. It is the very same institutions that cultivate market fairness, that also cultivate moral capabilities. Education, above all else, provides the foundation for a decent society, and a just, and non-oppressive marketplace. The more virtuous a person is, the less they require the market. Smith understands that there will be those who have no desire to participate in wide-spread commercial activity; among them are the intellectual and the legislator. For Smith, those individuals for whom consumer life holds no appeal, or those individuals who understand the inherent value of virtue, need not participate in the market. For them, the positive outcome of the market has already been achieved. The legislator then becomes the policy maker for the market and ensures that it runs smoothly upon a foundation of social institutions that cultivate virtue. The market can then continue to create universal opulence and makes the masses more virtuous.

However, Smith has not yet enumerated the nature of the legislator who is to guide society. Nor has he elaborated on his account of justice. Smith must therefore move from his discussion of the economic structure of society, to the institutions that maintain them. Smith must offer a theory of jurisprudence.

6

Justice and the Lectures on Jurisprudence

The Theory of Moral Sentiments ends with a promise that Smith will offer further texts elaborating the role of the state and the role of the legislator. It is clear that his plan was to create addenda to *TMS* because his first book would leave his readers with significant philosophical questions. In January of 1790, half a year before Smith died, the sixth edition of *TMS* was released with a new advertisement immediately following the title page. The final paragraph of the advertisement reads:

> In the last paragraph of the first Edition of the present work, I said, that I should in another discourse endeavour to give an account of the general principles of law and government, and of the different revolutions which they had undergone in the different ages and periods of society; not only in what concerns justice, but in what concerns police, revenue, and arms, and whatever else is the object of law. In the *Enquiry concerning the Nature and Causes of the Wealth of Nations*, I have partly executed this promise; at least so far as concerns police, revenue, and arms. What remains, the theory of jurisprudence, which I have long projected, I have hitherto been hindered from executing, by he same occupations which had till now prevented me from revising the present work. Though my very advanced

age leaves me, I acknowledge, very little expectation of ever being able to execute this great work to my own satisfaction; yet, as I have not altogether abandoned the design, and as I wish still to continue under the obligation of doing what I can, I have allowed the paragraph to remain as it was published more than thirty years ago, when I entertained no doubts of being able to execute every thing which it announced. (*TMS* advertisement.2)

There are several striking points in the above advertisement. First, given the fact that Smith had continually revised *TMS* since its publication, it is plausible to consider the project as having taken over thirty years to complete. That Smith was never fully satisfied with his work, even after it was published, is a testament to his philosophical disposition and his determination. Second, Smith's faith in his capacity for breadth of work is remarkable. It is impressive in itself that Smith would consider writing such a wide range of works. It is a remarkable statement about his intellect and his scholarly prowess that had he lived longer, he probably would have completed it all. Of course, he had a good role model. David Hume's own work habits were astounding. His large corpus including his multi-volume *History of England* must certainly have proved inspirational to his friend. Smith did avoid Hume's influence in one important way. Late in his life, Hume had been admonished by his publisher to lengthen his *History of England* but declined, explaining as his reasons, "I am too old, too fat, too lazy, and too rich".[56] It is clear that Smith never shared this sentiment about himself.

Smith was correct in his assumption that he would not complete his work on natural jurisprudence. Whatever fragments he had written were destroyed when he ordered his papers burned shortly before his death. Yet, once again, the study of Smith's work is assisted by the covert note-taking skills of his students. Two manuscripts exist recounting two of Smith's lectures on jurisprudence at the University of Glasgow. The first covers the years 1762-3 and is referred as *LJ(A)*, and the second covers the year 1766 and is referred to as *LJ(B)*.[57]

LJ(B) was actually the first to be discovered. It was found in 1895 in the possession of an Edinburgh lawyer. The writing is clear, neat, and obviously rewritten from a previous set of notes. This evidence suggests that the manuscript was being prepared for sale, as it was common at the time for bookshops to bind and sell professors' class notes. There is also a suggestion that the manuscript may have been transcribed from Smith's own notes that were passed on to his Glasgow replacement, but this would be hard to prove. *LJ(A)* was found, in fragments, in 1958, at an auction in Aberdeen. Scholars believe that these notes are based upon the same school session as those taken from his lectures on rhetoric, and, in fact, it is likely that the author of *LJ(A)* is the same as the author of *LRBL*.

The two sets of notes complement each other nicely. Because there are two, their claims can be tested for accuracy by comparison. This was never possible for *LRBL*. *LJ(B)* is shorter but has a wider range of topics. *LJ(A)* is substantially longer and provides added detail. The lectures contain few anecdotes, and little of the character of either *LRBL* or *TMS* is evident.

For the most part, the two lectures are used by scholars as a means to elaborate on topics covered in *WN*. The Glasgow edition of *WN* contains numerous references to *LJ* put together by the editors, and it is always interesting to cross reference the two works. In this regard, *LJ* has been treated as an appendix more than a work unto itself. For this reason, I will not present as lengthy an account of its contents as I have with Smith's other works. Instead, I will show how the two lectures may be used to supplement that which is already known.

Smith defines jurisprudence as "that science which inquires into the general principles which ought to be the foundation of the laws of all nations." (*LJ(B)*.1) As the definition suggests, the lectures are most helpful in reconstructing Smith's theory of governance and justice.

Smith's discussion of justice in *TMS* is surprisingly short and even then, it is paired with his discussion of beneficence. In *WN*, Smith has no discussion of justice proper, although he does concern himself with its expense. Smith devotes almost all of his energy to its discussion in *LJ*, but divides that discussion into categories regarding the rules of governance including a discussion of authority and parliamentary systems, of liberty, of rights, of marriage law, of voting behavior and other such areas. It is noticeable therefore, that for Smith, the term 'justice' refers to two different things, the first being the *virtue* of justice, and the second being the structure of the just state.

Traditionally, justice can be divided into two concerns: commutative justice and distributive justice. Distributive justice is that which is concerned with a fair "distribution" of resources within a society. It is that which ensures that the poor have access to a satisfactory level of goods and services, and also that which questions the distinction between equality of economic opportunity and the equality of economic result. There are, of course, systems in which the state is unconcerned with equality of any kind; equality is a choice. For example, Plato was not concerned with equality at all. In *Republic*, the Platonic Socrates argues that Justice is the harmonizing of the different strata in society. A just state is that state in which each citizen does that which he or she is best suited to do. Aristotle took equality into more consideration than Plato, but he argued that inequality was also important to cultivate. His notion of justice involved treating equals equally, but treating those who are not equal as equals was, for him, an example of injustice.

Those who are in favor of equality of result seek a situation in which, regardless of the means of achieving prosperity, all individuals end up with the same resources. In such a society, there is to be no economic class distinction or hierarchy of wealth. Communism is an example of a political theory devoted to this type of equality. Those who are in favor of equality of opportunity seek an equal starting point, and, assuming that all individuals abide by just rules of entitlement, whatever disparity in wealth results after the fact is regarded as fair. Smith's theory fits into the latter category. His concern for universal opulence is a concern for distributive justice, although universal in this sense does not mean egalitarian. In this regard, he seeks to foster equality of opportunity. His concern for the means by which the government should defray the costs of education and the cost of access to the courts of justice are all in the purview of distributive justice, as is his appeal to equity and common human decency in his discussion of wages. Other non-economic factors play into this concern, especially his concern for education. Smith's concern for the cultivation of sympathy can be viewed as a component of his concern for equality of opportunity as well.

Commutative justice is that which is concerned with redress of harm. Implicit in such a discussion is an understanding of what harm is, as well as the acceptable means of punishment. Whereas *WN* is primarily concerned with distributive justice, *TMS* is most concerned with commutative justice. *TMS* is also most concerned with justice as a virtue and not justice as the principle of ordering the state. Justice, as a virtue, is justice as an activity. The ability to adhere to the rules of justice must therefore be something that is in control of the moral agent, and must also be a product of decision-making capacities. In this regard, Smith argues that justice is of primary importance, and that it is "accurate in the highest degree, and admit[s] no exceptions or modifications." (*TMS* III.6.10)

TMS emphasizes the virtue of justice because the virtues are cultivated through Smith's moral psychology. At their root are the passions, and, as has been discussed in detail, temperance of the passions is the result of sympathy and the product of the imagination. Being virtuous is being in accordance with those sentiments that would be approved of by the impartial spectator, and as a result, the impartial spectator must play a role in the establishment of justice as well. Given the fact that the impartial spectator is fallible and shares human limitations, one must wonder how Smith might justify his faith in the precision of justice.

In this context, precision is justifiable because of a particular character of justice; it is a negative virtue. In regards to justice, Smith uses the term negative in three ways. First, according to Smith, one does not identify what justice is. Instead, one identifies that which justice isn't. One becomes aware of the rules of justice by experiencing acts of injustice and ruling out those acts that are regarded as unjust. It might therefore be suggested that if it were the case that no injustice was ever committed, the rules of justice would never be known.

A second way in which Smith identifies the negative character of justice is in respect to the way in which a person is to act justly. He writes:

> Mere justice is, upon most occasions, but a negative virtue, and only hinders us from hurting our neighbour. The man who barely abstains from violating either the person, or the estate, or the reputation of his neighbours, has surely very little positive merits. He fulfills, however, all the rules of what is particularly called justice, and does every thing which his equals can with propriety force him to do, or which they can punish him for not doing. We may often fulfill all the rules of justice by sitting still and doing nothing. (*TMS* II.ii.1.10)

Justice is negative in that refraining from hurting others or from violating their rights is all that is required. No *positive* action is required. A person is in accordance with justice even when he or she is not acting. According to Smith, justice should be of paramount concern because there is no justifiable motive for intentionally hurting or doing "evil" to others. (*TMS* II.ii.2.1) Interestingly, Smith continues this conversation with an eye towards self-interest. He remarks that the human perspective is such that one's own needs are far larger in one's own minds than are the needs of others, but that individuals must temper these feelings and "view ourselves not so much according to that light in which we may naturally appear to ourselves, as according to that in which we naturally appear to others." (*TMS* II.ii.2.2)

For Smith, man can only subsist in society. Each person requires the assistance of others, and social life demands some sort of reciprocity. (*TMS* II.ii.3.1) For this reason, justice is the "main pillar that holds up the whole edifice" of society. (*TMS* II.ii.3.3) He writes:

> In order to enforce the observation of justice, therefore, Nature has implanted in the human breast that consciousness of ill desert, those terrors of merited punishment which attend upon its violation, as the great safe-guards of the association of mankind, to protect the weak, to curb the violent, and to chastise the guilty. Men, though naturally sympathetic, feel so little for another, with whom they have no particular connexion, in comparison of what they feel for themselves, the misery if the one, who is merely their fellow creature, is of so little importance to them in comparison even of a small conveniencey of their own; they have it so much in their power to hurt him, and may have so many temptations to do so, that if this principle did not stand up within them in his defence, and overawe them into a respect for his innocence, they would, like wild beasts, be at all times ready to fly upon him; and a man would enter an assembly of men as he enters a den of lions. (*TMS* II.ii.3.4)

Smith's appeal to justice is a powerful one. It is a mixture of an appeal to benevolence – that feeling that one must respect and care for others – and an understanding that such altruistic sentiments are always placed in juxtaposition with one's own self-interestedness. Smith understands that in some sense, justice is care for the community, but Smith insists that it is harm towards individuals that inspires ire. Typical of Smith, utilitarian considerations are overshadowed by individual relationships. He writes:

> so when a single man is injured or destroyed, we demand the punishment of the wrong that has been done to him, not so much from a concern for the general interest of society, as from a concern for that very individual who has been injured... The concern which is requisite for this, in no more than the general fellow feeling which we have with every man merely because he is our fellow-creature. (*TMS* II.ii.3.11)

Smith's discussion of justice illustrates the role of the sentiments by concluding *TMS*'s discussion of justice with the claim that individuals are reticent in their acceptance of "excessive" penalties such as capital punishment. (*TMS* II.ii.3.11) Here Smith shifts into claims about policy, a rare occurrence in *TMS*. It illustrates that justice is negative in a third way. Whereas all virtues are cultivated by tempering passions through approval, justice is identified through spectator disapproval. Therefore, any conflict within the person who understands intellectually the import of capital punishment, but still feels a sentiment of regret or concern, must be taken very seriously. This regret or concern is a signal towards the presence of injustice.

TMS does not resolve this issue. There is little prescription to guide society in matters of policy or of particulars regarding the structure of the state. This is, of course, the nature of moral psychology as well as the method of the Newtonian didactic. The general principle is established – justice is abstention from harm to others – an account of the method of establishing the principle is provided – justice is established through the deliberations and disapproval of the impartial spectator – and the rest is left for another time. Naturally, the reader must turn to *WN* for more information, where from a legislative standpoint, Smith's discussion of justice are also surprisingly spare.

At this point we must consider the second type of justice, that of the mechanism of the just state. This is, of course, a form of commutative justice in that the mechanisms are designed to prevent and compensate harm, but the perspective is different. Rather than focus on the virtue that makes people act justly, Smith will focus on the laws that cultivate that virtue. Because justice is negative in character, and because justice may be realized simply by the lack of harm – recall that for Smith, a person is just even when they abstain from action – justice that is forced is as real as justice that is voluntary. Police enforcement of justice is no less just because the person who is being forced is not motivated to be just on his or her own. In this instance, intention means nothing, and such a characteristic leads Smith to be able to write, "a military government allows the strictest administration of justice" without, in fact, endorsing any kind of tyranny or fascism. *(LJ(B)*.45)

As in *WN*, the approach to justice in *LJ* is historical. In each instance, Smith provides an overview of the history of attitudes regarding the topic in question. This is further evidence of the Enlightenment belief that history is relevant to ethics and political philosophy. The rights and duties of both the sovereign and the citizen vary in different time-periods. His account begins with a rejection of the doctrine of social contract, and follows governmental structure through feudalism, monarchy, republicanism, and militaristic governments. For example, notice Smith's discussion of the possibility of assassination of royalty and political officials:

> Every attempt to overturn this power is in every nation considered as the greatest crime and is called high treason. It is observed that

there is a great difference between treason in monarchies and treason in republics. In the one it is an attempt on the kings person and in the other on the liberties of the people, from whence we may see how the maxim of assassination came to be established in republics, and not in monarchies. It is the interest of the monarchies that the person in authority be defended whatever his title or conduct be, and that no person be allowed in enquire into them. The laws of monarchy are therefore unfavourable to the assassination of tyrants. In a republic the definition of a tyrant is quite clear. He is one who deprives his people of their liberty, levies armies and taxes, and puts his citizens to death as he pleases. This man cannot be brought to a court of justice and therefore assassination is reckoned just and equitable. (LJ(B).79)

Notice that Smith's account of assassination is non-judgmental. He describes the conditions within the proper historical context and assumes that different types of governments have different rules.

How does *LJ* resolve the problem of ambiguity of harm as discussed above? Smith solves this problem by offering a clearer definition of the meaning of harm, and an elaborate system of classification. In *WN*, Smith tells us that justice is one of the duties of the sovereign, and that in this context, justice should be understood as "protecting, as far as possible, every member of society from the injustice or oppression of every other member of it". (V.i.b.1) *LJ* elaborates on this point by providing an enumeration of ways in which a person can be harmed by others: as a person in him or herself, as a member of a family, or as a member of a state. (*LJ(B)*.7, *LJ(A)* 1.10)) He explains that to be injured as a person is to be injured in body, reputation, or estate. To be injured as a member of the family is to be injured as a parent, a child, a spouse, a master or servant, or a guardian or pupil. To be injured as a member of the state, one is subjected to either disobedience or oppression depending on the context. (*LJ(B)*.7)

Smith further elaborates on each category within the above list. His discussion of being injured in reputation is paradigmatic and worth detailing. Smith states that the key to such injury is falsely representing someone as "an object of resentment or punishment". (*LJ(B)*.8) An example of such injury would be to falsely accuse someone or to "degrade him below his level of his profession". Smith further illustrates,

A physician's character is injured when we endeavour to perswade the world he kills his patients instead of curing them, for by such a report he loses his business. We do not however injure a man when we do not give him all the praise that is due his merit. We do not injure Sir Isaac Newton or Mr. Pope when we say that Sir Isaac was no better philosopher than Descartes or that Mr. Pope was no better poet than the ordinary ones of his own time. By these expressions we do not bestow on them all the praise that they deserve, yet we do them no injury, for we do not throw them below the ordinary rank of men in their own professions. (LJ(B).8)

Notice first that this injury requires positive action. It is not enough to refrain from offering due praise, one must actively cause harm in order to injure. Notice also that Smith implicitly distinguishes between accusation and criticism. To suggest that Pope is a mediocre poet is within the confines of Pope's profession. To be a literary figure is to openly subject oneself to review. Furthermore, the physician is only injured when one "falsely" accuses him or her of killing patients. This is also a necessary requirement since should it actually be true that a doctor is incompetent, individuals must preserve the ability to warn others.

Smith's account of harm is steeped in the legal method. Injury is determined by categorization. If there is no fitting category, then, presumably, there is no harm. Of course, it is the legislator's profession to review and adjust legal statutes to meet needs, but no court can condemn any action that is not against a particular law. This of course brings Smith to a discussion of rights, during which Smith argues there are two kinds, real rights, or rights over possessions and property, and personal rights. Of real rights there are four kinds: property, servitudes, pledges and exclusive privileges. (LJ(B).8) Property rights include rights over possessions that are taken by "stealth or violence". Servitudes are those rights one has to the properties of others such as the right of passage through a field or a road. Pledges refer to something that one has a right to but does not possess, such as pawns or mortgages, and exclusive privileges are those rights that are granted for a given amount of time. Smith cites an example of a book-seller having the right to an exclusive sale of a book for a particular number of years. *(LJ(B)*.10)

Of personal rights, Smith enumerates three. They are rights of: Contract, Quasi Contract and Delinquency. Right of contract is based on promises made and bound by "reasonable expectation" that the promise will be kept. Right of Quasi contract is that right a person has when turmoil engenders certain compensation necessary. Smith cites an example of a person finding a watch and returning it to its owner, and suggests that the finder is entitled to compensation for expenses in the process of recovery. Right of delinquency is the right to redress from damage done to a person through intent or neglect. *(LJ(B)* 10-11).

Smith indicates that this list of rights "make up the whole of a man's estate" *(LJ(B)* 11). It should be noted that this does not include civil rights such as the right to vote or the freedom of assembly. Certainly, Smith would be forced to place those particular rights within a historical context. There is therefore one remaining question, and that regards the origin of natural rights. Of this, Smith writes,

> The origin of natural rights is quite evident. That a person has a right to have his body free from injury, and his liberty free from infringement unless there be a proper cause, no body doubts. But acquired rights such as property require more explanation. Property and civil government very much depend on one another. The preservation of property and the inequality of possession first formed it, and the state of property must always vary with the form of government. *(LJ(B)* .11)

Here we see that Smith roots all rights in property. Recall that in *WN*, Smith founded property in labor and attached labor to liberty by arguing that it is "sacred and inviolable". (I.x.c.12). Recall also that Smith argues that perfect liberty is the ability for each person to choose his or her own profession. Of course, in economic terms, one's profession is one's sphere of labor. Therefore, choosing one's profession is really choosing the nature and product of one's labor.

For Smith, natural rights are intertwined with the free-market. Politics and economics are inseparable, and the nature of rights will vary historically depending on a state's economy. Smith is explicit about this fact in *WN*. By relating *WN* and *LJ*, we have elaborated further on Smith's claim that without economic freedom there is no political freedom. We have also made it clear that for Smith, the relationship between labor, rights and liberty is the foundation of justice.

Space does not allow elaboration on other topics in *LJ*. Readers of Smith are encouraged to use the lectures as a supplement to his work, but as always, caution is required. Smith did not endorse the lectures, and where there is conflict, Smith's published writings must always take precedence. It is clear from the discussion of justice, however, that these lectures are more helpful than confusing, and that they help provide detail when it is found to be necessary.

Thus, we end this chapter with a reminder that economic and political considerations require one another. This of course is the dominant claim in *WN*. In our discussion of justice, we see even more graphically that morality must complete the triad of the studies of human interaction. The virtue of justice is incomplete without the legal details that come with political and economic systems, but, of course, politics and economics can have no normative force if they are not rooted firmly in morality. It becomes most clear at the end of Smith's life that if one is to take his work seriously, one must also examine his plan of action. *TMS* and *WN* are incomplete without his discussion of law and government. It is terribly unfortunate that Smith was unable to complete his system, but with the assistance of what may be just two judicious students, Smith's work is, at least in some important way, finished.

7

Conclusion

Adam Smith died on July 17, 1790. He was 67 year old. He had no children, and bequeathed most of his estate to a distant relative. To the rest of the world, he bequeathed two best-selling books, and some scraps of unfinished writing. It would be unfair to suggest that after his death, *The Theory of Moral Sentiments* fell into obscurity, but it was certainly overshadowed by the impact made by its successor. *An Inquiry into the Nature and Causes of the Wealth of Nations* was the harbinger of a capitalist revolution that has changed economics and politics forever. Capitalism has revised the way humans look at identity and explanation. Motives are explained in terms of satisfaction of desires, and success is identified in terms of wealth and fame. The reduction of human beings into consumer machines is far from what Smith had in mind. It seems more in tune with Hobbes and Mandeville's vision of social interaction than that of the quirky, Scottish philosophy professor whose absent-minded manners charmed almost all who knew him

Smith had not predicted the industrial revolution. That, more than any other event, transformed the division of labor into a dominant method of manufacture. The dehumanizing impact of machinery glorified the most menial aspects of work and ignored the most social. Does this mean that Smith's work is obsolete? I do not think so. It does require that scholars be more sensitive to both Smith's original intent and his systematic approach to economics. However, I would suggest that Smith's work is as valuable today as it was when it was published.

Smith's work teaches a deep truth. An economics that is unconcerned with ethics is not amoral; it is immoral. A system of organization that divides agent from spectator to such an extent that it prevents sympathy is faulty and must be revised. A political organization that leaves many starving, uneducated, and unheard is no longer unified. The free-market must exist within a community; it should not replace it. There are those who suggest that social change must proceed by rejecting Smith and his followers. I, on the other hand, suggest that society will only improve if we reexamine Smith in the light of his actual message, and reject the distorted caricature of greed and quantification that much of contemporary economics has become.

In this book, I have tried to show that despite Smith's reputation as a proponent of the self-interested, cold, libertarian capitalism, he is, in fact, concerned with the cultivation of morality and the needs of the poor. I have also argued that Smith recognizes that the free-market is only an acceptable structure when it is supported by institutions designed to negate the inherently divisive and exploitative character of capitalism. If one were to start with Smith's economics, and either ignore or move backwards towards his moral theories, then perhaps one might see why purely *laissez faire* economics, and a society that is inherently competitive and uncaring, might be attributed to Smith. However, this is not how Smith saw his own work. This is not the chronology that Smith would have his readers follow. Smith spent the last years of his life revising *TMS*. The constant attention he paid it underscores its importance.

There are those who have used Smith for their own agenda. They have intentionally separated his economics from his morality, and have passed this method on to their students. They have justified neglect and exploitation in the name of a political system that is only defensible given a clear understanding and assent to a moral commitment to others. Smith had that commitment. He defended it clearly, and in the most sophisticated manner. He reminds us that we must care for each other and that we share responsibilities for the common good. He saw that the market was a helpful mechanism and spent much of his life defending that claim.

There are two projects that are currently incomplete. The first is in the realm of Smith scholarship. Recent work on Smith has emphasized the connectedness of his system, and has paid particular attention to his moral theory. This must be continued. Scholars must reclaim Smith's work from the legacy of the desperately false Adam Smith Problem. It must be made beyond question that *TMS* and *WN* are complementary and not exclusive. This requires regarding Smith as a philosopher first and an economist second. Since most of this type of research is done in the university, this project necessitates cross-disciplinary discussion and underscores the importance of philosophy, political science, and economics departments learning to communicate. Ironically, this lack of communication is a problem of sympathy. Such departments are currently too divided to understand each other. This should be rectified.

The second project requires a mixture of theory and practice. It is the project of reconceiving liberalism, the term for political systems that prioritize individual rights and allow citizens to choose their own conception of the good. That which is learned must then be applied and legislated. Of course, in many regards, this conversation already dominates contemporary political discourse. Concerns about welfare, affirmative action, the privatization of education, the role of choice in education, the place of religion in politics, and issues of diversity are all topics that Smith has addressed in his work, albeit obliquely. The irony is that Smith is not necessarily a supporter of the position that he is reputed to be. Perhaps his advice should once again be sought. It is just possible that Smith has more to say.

Endnotes

[1] Raphael, D.D. *Adam Smith.* (Oxford: Oxford University Press, 1985.
[2] For a discussion of the role of gender in Smith's work, see: Justman, Stewart. *The Autonomous Male of Adam Smith.* (USA: Oklahoma University Press, 1995).
[3] Ross, Ian Simpson. *The Life of Adam Smith.* (Oxford: Oxford University Press, 1995), 316.
[4] As quoted, *Ibid.,* pg. 334-335.
[5] As quoted, *Ibid.,* pg. 142.
[6] *Ibid.,* pg. 237.
[7] As quoted, *Ibid.,* Ross, pg. 226.
[8] *Ibid.,* pg. 210.
[9] *Ibid.,* pg. 192.
[10] As quoted *Ibid.,* pg. 336.
[11] *Ibid.,* pg. 406.
[12] *Ibid.,* pg. 257.
[13] As quoted *Ibid.,* pg. 376.
[14] *Ibid.,* pg. 244.
[15] *Ibid.,* pg. 402.
[16] *Ibid.,* pg. 214.

[17] Muller, Jerry Z. *Adam Smith In His Time and Ours* (Princeton: Princeton University Press, 1993), 21-22.
[18] As quoted, *Ibid.*, 21.
[19] *Ibid.*, 22.
[20] As quoted, *Ibid.*, 163
[21] Stewart, Dugald " Account of the Life and Writings of Adam Smith, LL.D", *Essays on Philosophical Subjects*. Edited by W.L.D. Wightman (Oxford: Oxford University Press, 1980), 270.
[22] West, E.G., *Adam Smith* (Indianapolis: Liberty Press, 1976), 53.
[23] Macintyre, Alasdair. *Whose Justice? Which Rationality?* (Notre Dame: University of Notre Dame Press, 1988), 248.
[24] Muller, 171.
[25] Haakonssen, Knud. *Natural Law and Moral Philosophy* (Cambridge: Cambridge University Press, 1996), 4.
[26] *Ibid.*, 7.
[27] Shaftesbury, Anthony Ashley Cooper, Third Earl of. *Characteristics of Men, Manners, Opinions, Times*. Edited by John M. Robertson. (Indianapolis: The Bobbs-Merrill Company, Inc., 1964), 180 – 181.
[28] Ross, pg. 54.
[29] See: Hutcheson, Francis. *An Inquiry into the Original of Our Ideas of Beauty and Virtue* (Virginia: Ibis Publishing, 1986)
[30] See, *Corr.*
[31] *EPS*, pg. 5
[32] *EPS*, pg. 7.
[33] Aristotle, *Met* 982b.
[34] Hume refers to objects and not events throughout his discussion of causation. A.J. Ayer argues that one term can be substituted for the other. For a concise discussion of Hume's theory of causation in the *Treatise*, and its relation to Hume's discussion of causation in *Enquiry Concerning Human Understanding and concerning the Principles of Morals*, see: Ayer, A.J. *Hume*. (Oxford: Oxford University Press, 1980), chapter 4.
[35] Peirce, C.S. "The Fixation of Belief" *Philosophical Writings of Pierce*. Edited by Justus Buchler. (New York: Dover Publications, 1955, pp. 5-22.
[36] Griswold, Charles L. Jr.'s *Adam Smith and the Virtues of Enlightenment.* (Cambridge: Cambridge University Press, 1999), especially pp. 48 – 58. The word is Griswold's. To understand its etymology, one need only divide it into its Greek components: *pro*

meaning toward, and *treptic* meaning turn. The definition, then, would be a turning towards something. In this context, Smith is turning the reader towards the community of 'we', but also guiding the reader towards a set of ethical principles.

[37] Mandeville, Bernard. *The Fable of the Bees or Private Vices, Public Benefits.* (Indianopolis: Liberty Press, 1988), vol. 1, pg. 324.

[38] Mandeville, vol. 1., pg 333.

[39] There are at least three ways in which to regard the liberal claim that individuals are somehow prior to the community. The first is an understanding at its most literal. Social contract theorists such as Hobbes and Locke saw the role of the state of nature as essential in justifying political normativity and the right of governance through consent. For such theorists, the shift from pre-social to social necessitated a voluntary agreement that granted political authority to others. Smith does not accept this point of view; he is not a social contract theorist. The second way of understanding the priority of individuals is as a priority of right over good, as in the work of John Rawls and Ronald Dworkin. This is more complex. Smith does not accept the possibility of rational adjudication without a context, and, therefore, it would be hard to argue for Smith's acceptance of, for example, a Rawlsian original position. However, Smith's theory of competition of religion does suggest that there is some manner in which right does trump substantive beliefs. This requires much more discussion than space allows. The third way of understanding individual priority is simply to suggest that there do exist certain natural rights that an individual may use to counter the authority of the state. In other words, there are certain inalienable rights that an individual may always hold claim to independent of the needs of the state. This too is complex, but it is certainly reasonable to suggest that Smith's notion of limited government does allow, in some sense, for this claim.

[40] There is a potential difficulty given this view. Since analogous emotions are always imperfect, the self-hatred would necessarily be of a lesser degree than the original hatred felt by the slave. It is therefore necessary for those who wish to convince the slave-owner to change his or her practices to ensure that the information which the slave-owner learns is powerful enough that the slave-owner will feel enough self-hatred to change his or her ways. This should be taken as a general observation regarding all oppressive relationships. The greatest

difficulty is rarely liberation. Escape and violence are often mechanisms in which to achieve freedom (although they do not guarantee permanence). It is much more difficult to convince the oppressors to understand the oppression and to change their ways. With this shift in attitude comes both liberation and prevention of further oppression.

[41] Haakonssen, Knud. *The Science of A Legislator* (Cambridge: Cambridge University Press, 1981),140.

[42] Griswold, 201.

[43] My discussion of Rawls borrows liberally from an earlier publication evaluating the various forms of reasoning in liberal theory. See: Weinstein, Jack Russell. "Guest Editor's Introduction: Critical Thinking and the Tradition of Political Philosophy" *Inquiry: Critical Thinking Across The Disciplines.* Vol. XVIII, No. 1 (Autumn 1998), Guest Edited by Jack Russell Weinstein, 12-13.

[44] In the interest of completeness, it is important to note the qualification that agents in the original position are concerned with the well-being of at least one member of a successive generation, but I do not believe that such a qualification has much impact on the discussion here.

[45] Rawls, John. *A Theory of Justice* (Cambridge University Press, 1971), 152-157.

[46] Such a criticism can be found in: Sandel, Michael J. *Liberalism and the Limits of Justice.* (Cambridge: Cambridge University Press, 1982).

[47] Rawls, 48.

[48] For a much more detailed account of the possibilities of flaws in the impartial spectator, as well as a more in-depth discussion of sympathy, see chapter three of: Weinstein, Jack Russell. *Adam Smith and the Problem of Neutrality in Contemporary Liberal Theory* (Ann Arbor: UMI Dissertation Services, 1997), UMI Number 9738666.

[49] The worker would most likely be male in this instance. In the Amish community, 'traditional' gender roles are strictly enforced.

[50] Hospers, John. "The Libertarian Manifesto" *Justice: Alternative Political Perspectives, second edition.* (Belmont: Wadsworth Publishing Company, 1992), 41.

[51] *Ibid.*, 47.

[52] Muller, 140. Emphasis in original.

[53] Here, I refer specifically to the 1980 Penguin Classics edition edited

by Andrew Skinner.

[54] This provides another interesting parallel with Rawls. Rawls also required a multi-generational line of connection in the original position. See note 44, above.

[55] For a more detailed discussion of Smith's comments on religion, see Weinstein, Jack Russell. "Religion and Justice in the work of Adam Smith." *Kontroversen, Zeitschrift für Philosophie, Wissenschaft und Gesellschaft.* Heft 9, 2000.

[56] Ross, 220.

[57] My discussion of the discovery of the manuscripts follows that of the introduction in *LJ*, pp 5 – 13.